MOVING FROM **SPOKEN**
TO WRITTEN
LANGUAGE WITH **ELLs**

This book is dedicated to the faculty and administration (both Rudy Gonzalez and Marsha Guerrero) at Morrison Elementary School in Norwalk, California. Morrison is a high-performing elementary school in a high-poverty area that has academically beat the odds over and over again on behalf of its diverse population of students (90 percent Latino, 27 percent ELL, and 77 percent Free/Reduced lunch). The school has received many accolades over the past six years, including being honored as a California Distinguished School in both 2008 and 2012. Morrison is also one of five public elementary schools in California to win the Title 1 Academic Achievement Award for five years in a row (2009 to 2013). Additionally, Morrison received the California School Board Association Golden Bell Award in 2012 for closing the achievement gap between their native English speakers and ELLs by using ELD/ ALD time. This school continues to inspire me, not just because of their deserved recognition, but because of the hard work and commitment that these teachers display on behalf of their students, the community, and each other. I have been honored to work with Morrison over the past five years as they refine their practices around meeting the needs of ELLs. Each time that I work with this group of teachers, they remind me that it is possible to beat the odds, and they continue to inspire me to work with other schools around that same mission.

MOVING FROM **SPOKEN** **TO** **WRITTEN** LANGUAGE WITH **ELLs**

Ivannia Soto

CORWIN
A SAGE Company

CORWIN
A SAGE Company

FOR INFORMATION:

Corwin
A SAGE Company
2455 Teller Road
Thousand Oaks, California 91320
(800) 233-9936
www.corwin.com

SAGE Publications Ltd.
1 Oliver's Yard
55 City Road
London EC1Y 1SP
United Kingdom

SAGE Publications India Pvt. Ltd.
B 1/I 1 Mohan Cooperative Industrial Area
Mathura Road, New Delhi 110 044
India

SAGE Publications Asia-Pacific Pte. Ltd.
3 Church Street
#10-04 Samsung Hub
Singapore 049483

Printed in the United States of America.

A catalog record of this book is available from the Library of Congress.

ISBN 978-1-4522-8036-3

Acquisitions Editor: Dan Alpert
Associate Editor: Kimberly Greenberg
Editorial Assistant: Cesar Reyes
Project Editor: Veronica Stapleton Hooper
Copy Editor: Janet Ford
Typesetter: C&M Digitals (P) Ltd.
Proofreader: Susan Schon
Indexer: Molly Hall
Cover Designer: Gail Buschman
Marketing Manager: Stephanie Trkay

This book is printed on acid-free paper.

SUSTAINABLE FORESTRY INITIATIVE
Certified Chain of Custody
Promoting Sustainable Forestry
www.sfiprogram.org
SFI-01268
SFI label applies to text stock

14 15 16 17 18 10 9 8 7 6 5 4 3 2 1

Contents

Acknowledgments

I want to acknowledge Whittier College for their ongoing support through faculty development grants of each of my Corwin books. Additionally, special thanks to my editor, Dan Alpert, for being supportive of my vision and guiding the progression of each Corwin book. Last, but not least, *un abrazo* to my mentor, Dr. Linda J. Carstens, for investing in me early on in my career, and continuing to stand beside me in further developing resources that started with our early work together in LAUSD: District 6 in California.

PUBLISHER'S ACKNOWLEDGMENTS

Corwin wishes to acknowledge the following peer reviewers for their editorial insight and guidance.

David Bautista, Education Administration
Woodburn School District
Woodburn, OR

Abbey S. Duggins, Assistant Principal for Instruction
Saluda High School
Saluda, SC

Carol Gallegos, ELA Curriculum Specialist
Hanford Elementary School District
Hanford, CA

E. Ann Markarian, EL Coordinator
Lucia Mar Unified School District
Arroyo Grande, CA

Mrs. Michelle D. Owen, Principal
Handy Elementary
Orange Unified School District
Orange, CA

Renee J. Ponce-Nealon, Kindergarten Teacher
Petaluma City School District
Petaluma, CA

Diane Senk, ELL Teacher
Pigeon River Elementary School
Sheboygan, WI

About the Author

 **Dr. Ivannia Soto** is associate professor of education at Whittier College, where she specializes in second language acquisition, systemic reform for English Language Learners (ELLs), and urban education. She began her career in the Los Angeles Unified School District (LAUSD), where she taught English and English language development to a population made up of 99.9 percent Latinos who either were or had been ELLs. Before becoming a professor, Dr. Soto also served the Los Angeles Unified School District as a literacy coach and district office administrator. She has presented on literacy and language topics at various conferences, including the National Association for Bilingual Education (NABE), the California Association for Bilingual Association (CABE), the New York State Association for Bilingual Education (NYSABE), and the National Urban Education Conference. As a consultant providing technical assistance for systemic reform for ELLs and Title III, Soto has worked with Stanford University's School Redesign Network (SRN) and WestEd, as well as a variety of districts and county offices in California. She is the coauthor of *The Literacy Gaps: Building Bridges for ELLs and SELs*, her first book with Corwin, and the author of a variety of articles on providing appropriate instructional access for ELLs. Her second book for Corwin, *ELL Shadowing as a Catalyst for Change* was published in 2012.

Introduction

As states across the country begin to contend with how to roll out the Common Core State Standards (CCSS) as the new benchmark for what students should know and be able to perform at each grade level, they also have to determine how to meet the needs of ELLs within a more rigorously and cognitively demanding set of expectations for all students. Currently, one out of every four students in the United States comes from an immigrant family, where most of the time children speak a language other than English (Ballantyne, Sanderman, & Levy, 2008). Similarly, whereas the general population grew by 7 percent in the decades between 1997 and 1998, and 2008 and 2009, the ELL population grew by 51 percent (Ballantyne et al., 2008). However until recently, the rapid growth in the number of ELLs has not been matched with sufficient knowledge about the best way to educate this population of students with the new grade-level academic expectations, especially within the academic mainstream.

The Elementary and Secondary Education Act (ESEA) suggests that all students, including ELLs, must have access to the core curriculum and meet specific academic targets (NCLB, 2002). As a result, many schools and districts are struggling with how to meet the linguistic needs of ELLs across all domains of listening, speaking, reading, and writing. Reading and writing, especially, are often areas where ELLs lag in achievement. Writing, specifically, is the most cognitively and linguistically demanding of the domains, as it is the culmination of speaking, reading, listening, plus syntax, grammar, and vocabulary development. Additionally, teachers are frequently not adequately prepared to teach writing across genres and content areas.

Basic writing programs create foundational writing skills, but the need for students to argue and explain using multiple sources and points of view is also expected within the CCSS; writing instruction needs to extend to those demands. For example, the genre of argumentative writing is a key focus area in the CCSS. All students are expected to *interpret, argue,* and *analyze*, before being able to address the genre of argumentative writing. Scaffolding these cognitive skills for ELLs is essential for them to access the academic demands of content area instruction. Linquanti and Hakuta (2012) agree that language and content must no longer be taught in isolation:

> the overlap between language and content has dramatically increased, particularly as a result of the focus on higher-order language uses in the new standards. In addition, the [Understanding Language] Initiative argues that this overlap brings with it an urgent need to attend to the particulars of instructional discourse in the disciplines. (p. 8)

Since the overlap between language and content increased, correspondingly, so does the need for preparation to prepare ELLs for the demands associated with writing across disciplines.

From Spoken to Written Language begins by presenting the research on the linkage between academic oral language and writing development, as well as how strategically using speaking to scaffold writing assists with closing the achievement gap between ELLs and their native English peers. The book specifically focuses on the literature regarding the need to create more oral language for ELLs in a mainstream classroom setting—with an emphasis on ELLs at higher levels of language proficiency (intermediate to advanced)—which can directly scaffold the writing tasks that are explicitly taught across the content areas. The book then unpacks a framework for teaching three specific genres of writing—argumentative, procedural, and narrative writing—along with a lesson plan guide and sample lessons. The text's language is user-friendly for classroom teachers, yet contains enough research to employ as a textbook in the university classroom or for professional development. Direct connections to the CCSS are also highlighted throughout the book.

The book is also applicable to classroom practice, as well as district and school reform efforts, with specific focus on ELLs in the mainstream classroom at the intermediate to advanced level. Teachers discover focused and detailed strategies and frameworks for altering instructional practice around using best scaffolding practices for ELLs incrementally; and administrators uncover how to increase academic achievement as schools implement these writing processes schoolwide. This book presents a user-friendly and accessible approach to teaching writing to ELLs within the CCSS. Whereas the rigor and expectations for this group of students have increased within this new reform movement, not much has been written regarding how pedagogy and practices should change in order to meet these expectations. *From Spoken to Written Language* explicitly calls out the scaffolds necessary to prepare ELLs for college and career expectations.

In my last book, *ELL Shadowing as a Catalyst for Change* (Soto, 2012), I presented the need for creating room for academic oral language development in classrooms. Specifically, that ELLs are oftentimes invisible and silent in school, and that in order to meet English language proficiency standards and provide access to the core curriculum, students need to be *required* to speak more than the two percent of a school day which is oftentimes expected of them (August, 2003). In this book, I extend the notion of how to directly use academic oral language development as a scaffold for the demands and rigor of writing. I developed detailed frameworks and lesson plans guides, based on the work of Pauline Gibbons's genre approach to teaching writing. Additionally, academic oral language development is embedded in writing lessons through the strategic teaching and use of Think-Pair-Share learning technique. In this book, I also directly show teachers how to use Think-Pair-Share to scaffold and extend into academic writing. Similarly, there is a focus on building background knowledge experiences, frequently using productive group work including Reciprocal Teaching, and participating in Socratic Seminar so that students have enough content knowledge for a written topic. Lastly, I incorporate the Frayer model to strategically teach vocabulary development so that students have a verbose vocabulary set with which to write.

The book is organized around two sections: (1) the role of academic oral language development as a scaffold for writing. The two chapters in this section introduce the research linkage between speaking and writing, as well as present the writing demands of the CCSS and how to scaffold them for ELLs; (2) the second section focuses on moving from speaking to writing across different genres—argumentation, procedural, and narration. Each of the chapters includes a sample lesson plan and graphic organizer template to use with your students. Please note that the lesson plans can be adapted for a variety of grade levels, but are targeted to a particular level (elementary, middle, or high school), to be inclusive of all grade levels holistically. The intent of the lesson plans is not necessarily that they are replicated as written (although they certainly can be), but rather that educators are given a model for how the strategies are used together, in order to scaffold the academic language demands of the CCSS. I highly encourage teachers to adapt and create their own lessons, using the strategies and resources included, as well as their own instructional materials.

The organization of the book is as follows:

- *At the beginning of each chapter,* the literature concerning meeting the instructional needs of ELLs, focusing in on the two domains of speaking and writing, and unpacking the writing demands of the CCSS is presented. Additionally, the research on the role and linkage between academic oral language development and writing across genres is described, along with practical strategies—Think-Pair-Share, Frayer model, and Socratic Seminar—to scaffold listening and speaking.

- *In the middle of the book* three different genres of writing—argumentation, procedural, and narration—are unpacked with a framework for taking students from speaking to writing, building background knowledge, and developing vocabulary so that students are adequately prepared for each writing approach. As each of the three genres of writing are unpacked, they are connected to the demands of the CCSS, and sample lessons are presented that are aligned to the common core.
- *At the end of the book,* a thorough index and lesson plan templates incorporating the CCSS are included.
- *Chapter Resources include:*

  o Lesson plan templates for the three genres of writing addressed in the CCSS; and
  o Academic language development strategy graphic organizers.

1 Academic Oral Language Development as a Scaffold for Writing in the Common Core

The Common Core State Standards (CCSS) movement requires teachers to shift their instructional practices in several significant ways, which in turn necessitates practice and intentionality. Some of these key shifts include embedding language development across the curriculum; an increase in oral language and multiple opportunities for speaking and listening; and an emphasis on collaboration, inquiry, and teamwork. These three shifts are described in the section that follows.

EMBEDDING LANGUAGE DEVELOPMENT ACROSS THE CURRICULUM

In our old paradigm of teaching language, we believed that we needed to teach the English Language Learner (ELL) to learn English first, before they were ready for academic content. At best, what we used to do to embed language was to integrate vocabulary as the overlap of language with our teaching. The figure below by Californians Together (2012) demonstrates

Figure 1.1 Old Paradigms

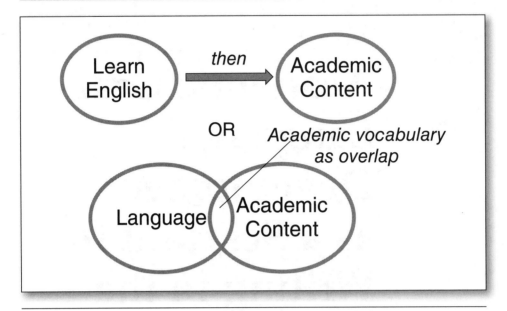

Source: Californians Together, 2012.

this old paradigm. Californians Together is a statewide coalition of parents, teachers, education advocates, and civil rights groups committed to securing equal access to quality education for all children.

Because many of our ELLs were not making adequate progress in both language and content, creating issues of access for this group of students, we simply cannot afford to teach these components of language one at a time, particularly with the rigorous expectations of the CCSS. Instead, as the figure 1.2 by Californians Together (2012) suggests, language must become central to all academic areas. These components of language may include instructional discourse, which connects to the emphasis on the listening and speaking standards within the CCSS, as well as expressing and understanding reasoning. In essence, we must find the academic language key to the content being taught, which includes academic oral language.

INCREASED FOCUS ON ORAL LANGUAGE AND MULTIPLE OPPORTUNITIES FOR SPEAKING AND LISTENING

In this way, the new speaking and listening demands of the CCSS require ELLs, who are oftentimes invisible and silent in classrooms, to participate in "academic discussions in one-on-one, small group, and whole-class

Figure 1.2 New CCSS Paradigm

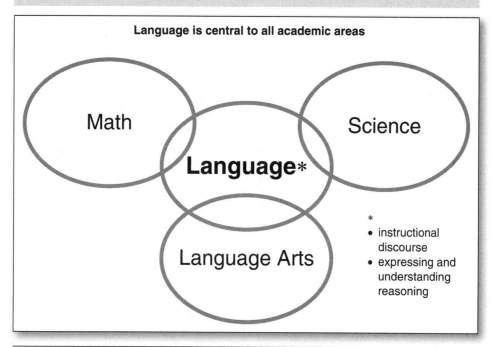

Source: Californians Together, 2012.

settings." Additionally, students need to "collaborate to answer questions, build understanding, and solve problems" (Common Core State Standards, 2013). This means that teachers must prepare intentional plans in order to elicit more opportunities for academic oral language development in the classroom setting. Oftentimes, however, educators may not realize the importance of incorporating academic talk into their classrooms, or they may not have been taught how to apprentice students into academic discourse, including active listening. The strategies introduced later in this section are designed to specifically assist teachers to successfully teach the speaking and listening standards.

Deborah Meier, visionary teacher, author, and founder of successful small schools in New York City and Boston suggests that "Teaching is listening, learning is talking" (http://deborahmeier.com/). The notion that students need to engage in more academic talk is at the heart of the CCSS movement, but it is essential to reorient our teaching in such a way that we systemically and intentionally begin to release more responsibility to students where they practice academic talk. In essence, we are reconceptualizing the last decade or so of educational policies and expectations, where the reverse was true: the teacher was talking and students were regurgitating information, not necessarily learning or internalizing concepts or content.

The College and Career Anchor Standard for Speaking and Listening #1, which is one of the overarching standards for speaking and listening, states, "Prepare for and participate effectively in a range of conversations and collaborations with diverse partners, building on others' ideas and expressing their own clearly and argumentatively" (CCSS, 2013). How will teachers operationalize the listening and speaking standards in order to ensure that students are apprenticed into the academic discourse patterns of school? The chart that follows is the progression of the Speaking and Listening Standards for Grades K–2 for the College and Career Anchor Standard for Speaking and Listening #1. The sections that are in bold are the manner in which this one standard builds from K–2 so that educators might note the increasing expectations for speaking and listening at the primary level alone. The section that follows addresses how this standard

Figure 1.3 Progression of the Speaking and Listening Standards for Grades K–2

Grade	Standards
K	1. Participate in collaborative conversations with diverse partners about **kindergarten topics and texts** with peers and adults in small and larger groups. a. Follow agreed-upon rules for discussions (e.g., listening to others and taking turns speaking about the topics under discussion). b. Continue a conversation through multiple exchanges.
1	1. Participate in collaborative conversations with diverse partners about **grade 1 topics and texts** with peers and adults in small and larger groups. a. Follow agreed-upon rules for discussions (e.g., listening to others **with care, speaking one at a time about the topics and texts under discussion**). b. **Build on others' talk in conversations by responding to the comments of others** through multiple exchanges. c. **Ask questions to clear up any confusion about the topics and texts under discussion.**
2	1. Participate in collaborative conversations with diverse partners about **grade 2 topics and texts** with peers and adults in small and larger groups. a. Follow agreed-upon rules for discussions (e.g., **gaining the floor in respectful ways**, listening to others with care, speaking one at a time about topics and texts under discussion). b. Build on others' talk in conversations by **linking their comments to the remarks of others**. c. **Ask for clarification and further explanation as needed about the topics and texts under discussion.**

progression may be explicitly taught in the classroom setting using the academic oral language development strategy called Think-Pair-Share.

Kindergarten to First Grade: Progression of College and Career Anchor Standards for Speaking and Listening #1

Within the Listening and Speaking Anchor Standard #1, the first progression noted in the above chart from Kindergarten to first grade is that conversations should be about grade-level material. Gone are the days of using reduced or watered-down curriculum and texts. ELLs are now expected to collaboratively participate in conversations about grade-level texts and materials. Therefore, in order to have ELLs access complex texts, this means that teachers must rely on instructional strategies and scaffolds even more. The second progression from Kindergarten to first grade is that in addition to "following agreed-upon rules for discussions," students are also expected to be able to "listen to others with care, speak one at a time about the topics and texts under discussion." Since ELLs, as well as most students, have not been expected to speak in the classroom setting, this progression needs to be modeled and practiced often. The third progression from Kindergarten to first grade is for students to "Build on others' talk in conversations by responding to the comments of others . . . ." With this standard, these notions need to be embedded into our teachings to attain success: that there is give and take in a conversation; and that we must truly be able and willing to listen to each other actively enough so that we can respond to our partner's comments, and not just exert our own ideas. The final progression from Kindergarten to first grade is, "Ask questions to clear up any confusion about the topics and texts under discussion." Students need to be apprenticed into how to ask appropriate questions, as well as different types of questions, which is a way to integrate Webb's Depth of Knowledge (Hess, Jones, Carlock, & Walkup, 2009) along with Bloom's Taxonomy, which is a classification of learning objectives within education addressed later in the book. Students also need to know how to ask questions appropriately, which can be taught using sentence stems.

First to Second Grade: Progression of College and Career Anchor Standards for Speaking and Listening #1

From first to second grade, the College and Career Anchor Standards progression for Speaking and Listening #1 increases again in terms of grade appropriate topics and texts. Again, the notion of integrating complex texts remains. The additional expectations include "following agreed-upon rules for discussion," and students must also be able to "gain the floor in respectful ways" (CCSS, 2013). Accordingly, the hidden curriculum of academic discourse must be explicitly taught so that students learn to not talk over one another, as well as how to disagree respectfully. Notice that this also becomes a lifelong skill essential for conversations in college discussions or career interactions.

Additionally, the progression in Listening and Speaking for Anchor Standard #1 from first to second grade includes "linking [student] comments to the remarks of others" (CCSS, 2013). The notion of actively listening to a partner's response so that one can find similarities in ideas is essential to success with this portion of the second grade standard. Lastly, "ask[ing] for clarification and further explanation as needed about the topics and texts under discussion" (CCSS, 2013) is the final progression from the first grade to the second grade with the Anchor Standard #1 for Listening and Speaking. Clarification is similar to the notion of asking questions in the first grade, but is a slight increment nonetheless, as questions in the first grade might be more about factual content, whereas clarification in the second grade might lend itself to thinking more deeply about an issue or question.

Educators should persist in this analysis of the progression of the Listening and Speaking Anchor Standards for all grade levels so that the shift in the expectations and important scaffolds necessary to teach these standards are embedded explicitly. The following section links the expectations within the listening and speaking standards to academic oral language development strategies which assist with supporting their incorporation in the classroom.

Linking the Listening and Speaking Standards to Strategies

One way to apprentice students to move from one-on-one, small group, and whole group discussion demands of the Common Core is to use academic oral language development strategies as scaffolds. According to many linguists, academic language is not natural language and must be explicitly taught. As previously discussed, the Understanding Language Initiative (2012) suggests that "the overlap between language and content has dramatically increased . . . this overlap brings with it an urgent need to attend to the particulars of instructional discourse in the disciplines." Specific strategies that assist ELLs with academic oral language development, as well as building background knowledge across disciplines, are introduced in the following section using academic oral language development strategies, including Think-Pair-Share, Reciprocal Teaching, and Socratic Seminar.

ONE-ON-ONE ORAL EXCHANGES: THINK-PAIR-SHARE STRATEGY

Unlike the partner-talk method, which is a briefer opportunity for academic talk, the Think-Pair-Share approach calls for teachers to embed specific academic oral language development scaffolds, including: 1) devising open-ended questions, which require longer responses and higher order thinking; 2) think time for students to carefully develop and support their responses; 3) requiring speaking and listening, as ELLs both share their own response with a partner, and listen carefully to their partner's response before writing down a response; and 4) coming to consensus regarding what kind of response is shared with the entire class. Think-Pair-Share allows ELLs to be more confident when they share out with a smaller group or during a whole-class discussion, and can also be used as a scaffold for writing (which is addressed later in this section).

Think-Pair-Share Graphic Organizer

The graphic organizer in Figure 1.4, which is also in the Appendix, is a way to begin to organize and include Think-Pair-Share into one's classroom practice. In the first column, a teacher looks at the CCSS objective and assessment information for the lesson in order to strategically determine the open-ended questions they want their students to discuss. In doing so, we ensure that students are focused and talking about the right things. It is also important to design questions ahead of time so that student conversations are purposeful and lead to speaking and writing outcomes desired at the end of the lesson and/or unit.

Designing Open-Ended Questions Using Depth of Knowledge Matrix

Figure 1.5 demonstrates Webb's (2002) groupings of tasks that reflect different levels of cognitive expectation of the depth of knowledge (DOK) required for success with a cognitive task. Notice some of the words used in the center of each of the four levels: Recall, Skill/Concept/ Strategic Thinking and Extended Thinking.

The verbs in the center alone are not enough to assign a DOK level. Teachers must also consider the complexity of the task and/or information, depth of prior knowledge for students at the grade level, and the mental processes used to satisfy the requirements set forth in the objective of the lesson/unit. This is the shift from a verbs only approach, to a more complex matrix that combines Bloom's Taxonomy (Bloom, Engelhart, Furst, Hill, &

Figure 1.4   Think-Pair-Share With Academic Language Stems

Question (Open-ended)	What I Think (Speaking)	What My Partner Thought (Listening)	What We Thought (Consensus)
What happened at the beginning of the story?			
What happened in the middle of the story?			
What happened at the end of the story?			

Source: Adapted from Soto, 2012.

Figure 1.5 Depth of Knowledge

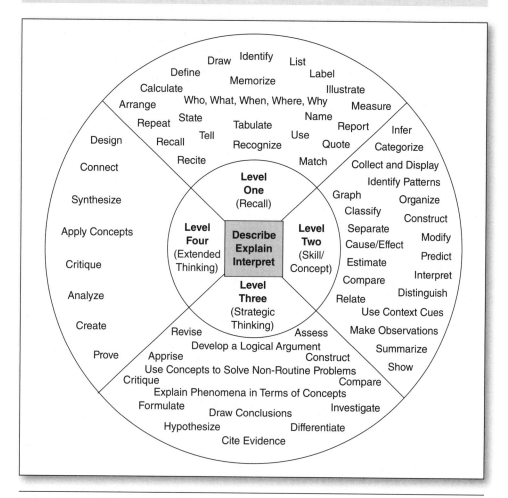

Source: Webb, 2012.

Krathwohl, 1956) with Smarter Balanced Depth of Knowledge levels, as demonstrated in Figure 1.6, which was developed by Karin Hess and colleagues (Hess et al., 2009).

This chart demonstrates the shift from previous theories usually applied in isolation (e.g., Costa's Levels of Thinking and Bloom's Taxonomy), to a combination of the four levels of the CCSS integrated with those previous ideas. Before, using only Bloom's Taxonomy (1956), students would progress from the simple to the more complex traveling downward in the chart. Combining Bloom's Taxonomy with the Smarter Balanced Assessment Depth of Knowledge levels, one can see how students can progress to deeper levels at each stage of Bloom's Taxonomy (Hess et al., 2009).

Figure 1.6 Applying Webb's DOK Levels to Bloom's Taxonomy of Educational Objectives (Karin Hess)

ELA/Soc St Examples	Webb's Depth of Knowledge Levels			
Bloom's Taxonomy	Level 1 Recall and Reproduction	Level 2 Skills and Concepts	Level 3 Strategic Thinking/Reasoning	Level 4 Extended Thinking
Knowledge Define, duplicate, label, list, memorize, name, order, recognize, relate, recall, reproduce, state	• List/generate ideas for writing or research • Recall, recognize, or locate basic facts, ideas, principles, concepts • Identify/describe key figures, places, or events in a particular context			
Comprehension Classify, describe, discuss, explain, express, identify, indicate, locate, recognize, report, restate, review, select, translate	• Write a simple sentence • Select appropriate word(s) to use in context when meaning is evident • Identify or describe characters, setting, plot, problem, solution • Describe or explain: who, what, where, when	• Determine or recognize main idea/ generalizations • Take and organize notes around common ideas/topics • Summarize ideas/ events • Make basic inferences or logical predictions from text • Explain relationship/ cause-effect	• Write full composition using varied sentence types & structures to meet purposes • Explain, generalize, or connect ideas using supporting evidence • Make inferences about theme or author's purpose	• Write full composition demonstrating synthesis & analysis of complex ideas • Compare multiple works by same author, across time periods, genres, etc.

ELA/Soc St Examples	Webb's Depth of Knowledge Levels			
Bloom's Taxonomy	Level 1 Recall and Reproduction	Level 2 Skills and Concepts	Level 3 Strategic Thinking/Reasoning	Level 4 Extended Thinking
Application Apply, choose, demonstrate, dramatize, employ, illustrate, interpret, practice, schedule, sketch, solve, use, write	• Apply spelling, grammar, punctuation, conventions rules in writing • Use structures (pre/ suffix) or relationships (synonym) to determine word meaning • Use resources to edit/ revise	• Write paragraph using a basic structure or template • Edit final draft for mechanics and conventions • Use context clues to determine meaning • Use text features to find information	• Edit final draft for meaning/ progression of ideas • Apply a concept in other/ new contexts • Support ideas with examples, citations, details, elaboration, quotations, text references	• Define and illustrate common social, historical, economic, or geographical themes and how they interrelate
Analysis Analyze, appraise, calculate, categorize, compare, criticize, discriminate, distinguish, examine, experiment	• Identify specific information contained in maps, charts, tables, graphs, or diagrams	• Analyze a paragraph for simple organizational structure • Determine fiction/ nonfiction; fact/ opinion • Describe purpose of text features • Identify use of literary devices	• Analyze an essay • Compare information within or across text passages • Analyze interrelationships among text elements, situations, events, or ideas • Analyze use of literary devices	• Analyze multiple works by the same author, across time periods, genres • Analyze complex/ abstract themes

Continued

Figure 1.6 (Continued)

ELA/Soc St Examples	Webb's Depth of Knowledge Levels			
Bloom's Taxonomy	Level 1 Recall and Reproduction	Level 2 Skills and Concepts	Level 3 Strategic Thinking/Reasoning	Level 4 Extended Thinking
Synthesis Rearrange, assemble, collect, compose, create, design, develop, formulate, manage, organize, plan, propose, set up, write	• Brainstorm ideas, concepts, or perspectives related to a topic		• Synthesize information within one source or text • Develop a model for a complex situation	• Synthesize information across multiple sources or texts • Given a situation/problem, research, define, & describe the situation/problem and provide alternative solutions
Evaluation Appraise, argue, assess, choose, compare, defend, estimate, judge, predict, rate, select, support, value			• Cite evidence and develop a logical argument for concepts • Make & support generalizations, using text evidence	• Gather, analyze, & evaluate information to draw conclusions • Evaluate relevancy, accuracy, completeness of information from multiple sources

Source: Hess et al., 2009.

For example, as shown in the figure above, the concept of remembering information only relates to the first depth of knowledge level. In contrast, evaluation does not relate to either of the first two levels of depth of knowledge, hence the two blank boxes, so educators must move to strategic and extended thinking to develop students' questions and assignments at these levels. This table, which is found in the Smarter Balanced Content Specifications for ELA (English Language Arts), is a useful aid for guiding the development of assignments and assessments at different depth of knowledge levels, including open-ended questions for Think-Pair-Share. Each step within Think-Pair-Share, including the development of questions alongside the Depths of Knowledge matrix, must be planned for explicitly by the teacher ahead of time in order for language benefits to occur. As such, teachers must not only apprentice students into the listening and speaking expectations of working with others, but also provide ELLs with a practice "talking round" where student thinking becomes more specific and precise via the academic talk and expression/solidification of ideas.

Connection Between Think-Pair-Share and CCSS Listening and Speaking Standards

Notice also the explicit connections of Think-Pair-Share to the standards addressed below. The highlighted areas demonstrate the connections between Think-Pair-Share and the CCSS for Listening and Speaking.

During Think-Pair-Share interactions, students are engaged in collaborative conversations, where they learn how to listen to each other with care, as well as how to take turns when speaking. The Think-Pair-Share graphic organizer, which has multiple slots on a page, and the last portion of the organizer, the *consensus/what we will share* section, in particular, allows students to continue the conversation through multiple exchanges, further justifying and clarifying their thinking. Along with justifying responses, students should be encouraged to incorporate textual evidence, and can be taught the following textual evidence sentence starters.

With appropriately designed follow-up questions by the teacher, students can also deepen/solidify their understanding of the content taught. These follow-up questions should also be carefully constructed.

Teaching Active Listening

Since active listening is not something that is typically taught in classrooms (until students get in trouble for not listening), ELLs can benefit greatly from active listening stems that require responses to paraphrase (see below and in Appendix). Additional building on partner responses

Figure 1.7 Connection Between Think-Pair-Share and CCSS Listening and Speaking Standards

Grade	Standards

K	1. Participate in collaborative conversations with diverse partners about kindergarten topics and texts with peers and adults in small and larger groups.
	    a. Follow agreed-upon rules for discussions (e.g., listening to others and taking turns speaking about the topics under discussion).
	    b. Continue a conversation through multiple exchanges.

1	1. Participate in collaborative conversations with diverse partners about Grade 1 topics and texts with peers and adults in small and larger groups.
	    a. Follow agreed-upon rules for discussions (e.g., listening to others with care, speaking one at a time about the topics and texts under discussion).
	    b. Build on others' talk in conversations by responding to the comments of others through multiple exchanges.
	    c. Ask questions to clear up any confusion about the topics and texts under discussion.

2	1. Participate in collaborative conversations with diverse partners about Grade 2 topics and texts with peers and adults in small and larger groups.
	    a. Follow agreed-upon rules for discussions (e.g., gaining the floor in respectful ways, listening to others with care, speaking one at a time about topics and texts under discussion).
	    b. Build on others' talk in conversations by linking their comments to the remarks of others.
	    c. Ask for clarification and further explanation as needed about the topics and texts under discussion.

stems can also be used to apprentice students into collaborative speaking experiences. Each of the academic language stems below should be introduced to fit the purpose of the language situation undertaken (i.e., when teaching about textual support, introduce and model the textual support sentence stems). Namely, all of academic language stems should not be posted at once, without explicit instruction and modeling regarding how to use each. Some teachers also choose to laminate and place the academic language stems on students' desktops so that they are more likely to use them in both oral and written responses throughout the day. This allows teachers to hold students accountable to academic talk. These academic oral language stems can then be extended into academic writing as students now know how to begin an academic conversation that mirrors academic expectations for writing.

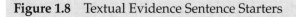

Figure 1.8 Textual Evidence Sentence Starters

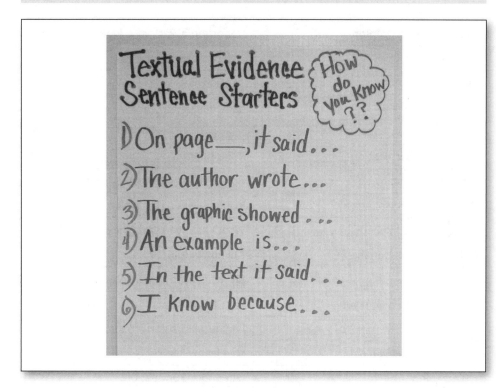

Collaborative Conversation via Think-Pair-Share

Each step in the Think-Pair-Share process explicitly teaches ELLs what participation in collaborative conversations requires from them. As suggested previously, students are required to think through the open-ended question or prompt, are given enough think time to write down their response (with an additional scaffold of academic language development stems for written and spoken language), and then are required to actively listen to their partner's response so that they might be able to connect or build on the conversation. The additional time spent explicitly teaching academic oral language development both allows ELLs to make deeper meaning around content and also allows them to practice important language skills needed to be successful within the CCSS.

Think-Pair-Share in the Primary Grades

The cards below (also found in the Appendices) can be used with students in the primary grades, as the younger students learn to take turns. The visual of the mouth reminds younger students when it is that they should be speaking and when they should be listening. The color-coding

Figure 1.9 Language Strategies for Active Classroom Participation

Expressing an Opinion	Reporting a Partner's Idea
___ concluded that . . .	____ indicated that . . .
I think/believe that . . .	____ pointed out to me that . . .
It seems to me that . . .	____ emphasized that . . .
In my opinion . . .	
Asking for Clarification	**Paraphrasing**
What do you mean?	So you are saying that . . .
Will you explain that again?	In other words, you think . . .
I have a question about that.	What I hear you saying is . . .
Soliciting a Response	**Acknowledging Ideas**
What do you think?	My idea is similar to/related to
We haven't heard from you yet.	____'s idea.
Do you agree?	I agree with (a person) that . . .
What answer did you get?	My idea builds on ____'s idea.
Disagreeing	**Offering a Suggestion**
I don't agree with you because . . .	Maybe we could . . .
I got a different answer than you.	What if we . . .
I see it another way.	Here's something we might try.
Affirming	**Holding the Floor**
That's an interesting idea.	As I was saying . . .
I hadn't thought of that.	If I could finish my thought . . .
I see what you mean.	What I was trying to say was . . .

Source: Adapted from Kinsella & Feldman, 2005.

is an additional visual scaffold for when students should speak—green, which is for go and speak while the listening card is red, for stop and listen. These cards can be photocopied in red and green to remind students of each of the moves within Think-Pair-Share.

An additional tool that can be used in the primary grades to apprentice younger students to the expectations of Think-Pair-Share is the Partner Chant illustrated below (Adapted from Mesa, 2011). Notice that the chant

Figure 1.10 Think-Pair-Share Cards for Primary Grades

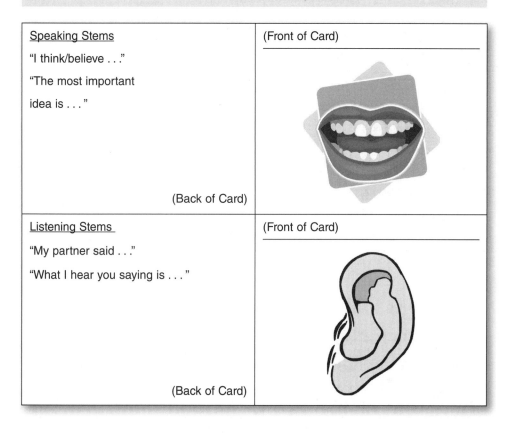

Speaking Stems	(Front of Card)
"I think/believe . . ."	
"The most important	
idea is . . ."	
(Back of Card)	
Listening Stems	(Front of Card)
"My partner said . . ."	
"What I hear you saying is . . ."	
(Back of Card)	

highlights each of the steps in Think-Pair-Share, including sitting in close proximity; looking at your partner when they are speaking (as a sign of respect and active listening); speaking with appropriate volume when sharing (which needs to be taught, perhaps using the volume dial on a radio); and then turning to the whole group to share the information. The notion of using polite voices, sharing one's thinking, and learning from each other are benefits of using this tool to acclimate students to the expectations of Think-Pair-Share. It further connects to the listening and speaking standards, including "listening to each other with care" and "speaking one at a time about the topics and texts under discussion." The chant can be posted in the room and sung when first introducing Think-Pair-Share to the class.

Metacognition and Think-Pair-Share

Once the appropriate questions are constructed for Think-Pair-Share (based on the standard, assessments, and/or objectives of the lesson), the

Figure 1.11 Partner Chant: Think-Pair-Share

Eye to eye

Knee to knee

Sit right here and learn from me

We'll speak with voices polite indeed

To share our thinking

About books we read

Our partner's thoughts can help us learn

The signal will tell us

It's time to turn

Source: Adapted from Mesa, 2011.

Figure 1.12 Metacomprehension Skills Across Content Areas

ELA/ELD Comprehension	History/SS Analysis	Mathematics Problem-Solving	Science Inquiry
Determining importance	Chronological and spatial thinking	Make an organized list Solve a simpler problem	Investigating
Inferring	Identifying and interpreting	Solve a similar problem	Interpreting
Making connections	Connecting present to the past	Find a pattern	Interpreting
Predicting	Historical interpretation	Predict and test	Predicting
Questioning	Posing relevant questions	Write an equation	Hypothesizing Questioning
Summarizing Synthesizing	Research, evidence, and point of view	Make a model or act it out	Communicating
Visualizing	Making visual representations	Draw a diagram or picture Make a table or graph	Observing

Source: Carstens, 2003.

students think through the question carefully, justify their opinion with perhaps one or more textual references (this also affords an opportunity for a second or third reading of a text), before writing down their own response in the second column of the Think-Pair-Share organizer. Again, students should use one of the academic language stems to assist with beginning their response. This allows the student, especially an ELL, to focus on the content while they internalize the language. The teacher should also present ample modeling of the metacognition used when thinking through and writing down one's response. Metacognition can be modeled by using a think aloud example, where the teacher shares her thinking processes out loud with the class. The following metacomprehension chart can be used as a guide regarding the key comprehension skills across content areas.

The example that follows connects to the content area of English Language Arts/English Language Development (ELA/ELD) Comprehension and the subskill area of Determining Importance. The conversation below captures a teacher's modeling of her metacognitive response to the question: In the 1993 book *Stellaluna* by Janell Cannon, what happened at the beginning, middle, and end?

Notice that if open-ended questions are carefully preplanned and designed for Think-Pair-Share, the responses can become a summary, or a longer writing selection, around a particular topic or text.

When first introducing Think-Pair-Share, if the teacher selects a simple text, perhaps one which has already been read to the class, it helps the ELLs focus on learning the strategy first. Then, when students are comfortable with the strategy, they can practice Think-Pair-Share with a more rigorous or grade-level text. Some teachers also elect to try the strategy with personal questions first, such as "What was the highlight of your weekend?"

Active Listening During Think-Pair-Share

In the above example, once students write down their individual responses, they can now work with a partner to actively listen to their beginning, middle, and end responses. During the listening segment of Think-Pair-Share, it is important that students actively listen to their partner's response by not trying to both listen and write at the same time. Instead, each partner should put down their pen or pencil, sit in close proximity to their partner so that they can hear them, and attend to the discussion by looking at them (note: please be aware of cultural differences and distinctions here where looking someone directly in the eye may be considered disrespectful). Notwithstanding, the academic and American expectations for active listening should be explicitly taught during the listening segment of Think-Pair-Share.

Figure 1.13 Think-Pair-Share With Academic Language Stems

Question (Open-ended)	What I Think (Speaking)	What My Partner Thought (Listening)	What We Thought (Consensus)
What happened at the beginning of the story?	*At the beginning of the story, Stellaluna, a baby fruit bat, gets separated from her mother during an owl attack. She ends up being raised by a mother bird and tries to fit in.*		
What happened in the middle of the story?	*Although she is accepted by the birds, Stellaluna never feels at home or herself because she physically looks different and does things differently (hangs instead of perches).*		
What happened at the end of the story?	*In the end, Stellaluna reunites with her mother and realizes that she isn't a bird, but a bat. She realizes that she can accept herself as a bat and appreciate the differences of birds who took her in.*		

Source: Adapted from Soto, 2012.

In order to ensure that a student adequately understood his or her partner's response, she or he should orally paraphrase the message to his/ her partner, before writing it down on paper. Once the students receive permission from their partners that the information was accurately understood, they may then write down their partner's summary in the column labeled "What my partner thought" in Figure 1.13. It is important to note that a summary or paraphrase of a partner's response should be taken down, not a transcription. Students should also not take down a response while a student is speaking, as most people cannot both listen carefully and write at the same time.

By summarizing and paraphrasing oral responses, the Think-Pair-Share strategy also reinforces important reading comprehension skills, as listening is a scaffold for reading (i.e., when we listen, we use similar processes as when we read).

Consensus/Sharing Out With the Whole Class

The final column of the Think-Pair-Share graphic organizer requires that students give careful consideration to what they share out with the whole class. Once again, students are encouraged to think through their individual and partner's responses in order to select the best response to share with the group. This process allows students to feel more confident about sharing out with the whole group, because together they have four options they can select for a response to the last column:

1. Share their own response and *justify why* it was the best response by identifying evidence;

2. Share their partner's response and *justify why* it was the best response by identifying evidence;

3. Combine both responses and *justify why* by identifying evidence; or

4. Come up with a whole new response from a new reading of the text and/or from the partner conversation, and *justify why* by identifying evidence.

Notice that each of the options in the "What we will share" section of the graphic organizer ensures that students are confident in their responses, and have thought deeply and critically about the question. Students should not just share their partner's response because "it was better," but instead must *justify* their thinking and selection of responses. Each of these moves within the Think-Pair-Share exercise builds collaboration and ensures understanding of important content, especially when open-ended questions are planned for carefully.

Figure 1.14 Think-Pair-Share With Academic Language Stems

Question (Open-ended)	What I Think (Speaking)	What My Partner Thought (Listening)	What We Thought (Consensus)
What happened at the beginning of the story?	*At the beginning of the story, Stellaluna, a baby fruit bat, gets separated from her mother during an owl attack. She ends up being raised by a mother bird and tries to fit in.*	*What I hear you saying is that Stellaluna gets separated from her mama bat and is raised by a mother bird instead. She struggles to be like her new family.*	
What happened in the middle of the story?	*Although she is accepted by the birds, Stellaluna never feels at home or herself because she physically looks different and does things differently (hangs instead of perches).*	*Because she's a bat and is being raised by birds, Stellaluna feels different, but can't quite figure out why she does things differently like hanging instead of perching.*	
What happened at the end of the story?	*In the end, Stellaluna reunites with her mother and realizes that she isn't a bird, but a bat. She realizes that she can accept herself as a bat and appreciate the differences of birds who took her in.*	*Stellaluna figures out why she is different when she reunites with her mother, who is a bat. She comes to accept her time with the birds, but also appreciates understanding why she is so different.*	

Source: Adapted from Soto, 2012.

Figure 1.15   Think-Pair-Share With Academic Language Stems

Question (Open-ended)	What I Think (Speaking)	What My Partner Thought (Listening)	What We Thought (Consensus)
What happened at the beginning of the story?	At the beginning of the story, Stellaluna, a baby fruit bat, gets separated from her mother during an owl attack. She ends up being raised by a mother bird and tries to fit in.	What I hear you saying is that Stellaluna gets separated from her mama bat and is raised by a mother bird instead. She struggles to be like her new family.	We both thought that it must have been hard to be separated from our families and struggle to be like our new family.
What happened in the middle of the story?	Although she is accepted by the birds, Stellaluna never feels at home or herself because she physically looks different and does things differently (hangs instead of perches).	Because she's a bat and is being raised by birds, Stellaluna feels different, but can't quite figure out why she does things differently like hanging instead of perching.	We both thought it would be hard to try to figure out why we do things so differently and not be fully part of a family because of it.
What happened at the end of the story?	In the end, Stellaluna reunites with her mother and realizes that she isn't a bird, but a bat. She realizes that she can accept herself as a bat and appreciate the differences of birds who took her in.	Stellaluna figures out why she is different when she reunites with her mother, who is a bat. She comes to accept her time with the birds, but also appreciates understanding why she is so different.	We both thought it was great that Stellaluna had this experience in two different families, and learned different ways of doing things.

Source: Adapted from Soto, 2012.

EMPHASIS ON COLLABORATION, INQUIRY, AND TEAMWORK

Group Work Essentials

Before moving from one-on-one to small group expectations for collaboration, it is important to highlight some group work essentials as well as connect group work to both language benefits and the Listening and Speaking Standards. The CCSS Listening and Speaking Anchor Standard #1 suggests, "The CCSSs recognize that students need to develop skills to *collaborate* in academic work—skills for teamwork, *active* and *skillful* participation in discussions, and inquiry-based collaboration." Again, apprenticing students from academic discussions that are one-on-one (as with Think-Pair-Share), to small group (as with Reciprocal Teaching), and to whole group (as with Socratic Seminar), takes modeling, structure, and practice in order for rich and rigorous conversations to ensue.

In tandem with the benefits of collaboration, including "answering questions, building understanding, and solving problems," it is important to note that collaboration and group work are not automatic or natural—they also must be taught explicitly. As we all know or have experienced, not all group work is productive or collaborative, especially if we are not explicit in our expectations. If group worthy tasks are not designed by teachers, or if we do not adequately lay out group norms, the benefits quickly diminish.

Some important guidelines to remember regarding productive group work come from Pauline Gibbons (2002), in her text *Scaffolding Language, Scaffolding Learning* where she lays out eight characteristics of productive group work.

These eight characteristics of group work can be used as a preparation manual (see planning guide on page 30) when designing and planning for

---

Figure 1.16   Common Core Connection

Speaking and Listening

- An important focus of the speaking and listening standards is **academic discussion** in **one-on-one, small group, and whole-class settings**.
- Formal presentations are one important way such talk occurs, but so is the more informal discussion that takes place as **students collaborate to answer questions, build understanding, and solve problems**.

Source: NGA & CCSSO, 2010.

Figure 1.17 Pauline Gibbons, Chapter 2, "Speaking"

Characteristics of Effective Group Work for ELL Students (pages 20–28)	
1. *Clear and explicit instructions are provided.*	5. *The task is integrated with a broader topic.*
2. *Talk is necessary for the task.*	6. *All children are involved.*
3. *There is a clear outcome.*	7. *Students have enough time.*
4. *The task is cognitively appropriate.*	8. *Students know how to work in groups.*

Source: Gibbons, 2002.

Figure 1.18 Eight Characteristics of Productive/Effective Group Work

1. **Clear and explicit instructions are provided**—instructions regarding the academic task and classroom environment expectations should be laid out carefully. Otherwise, frustration by both the teacher and student can ensue.

2. **Talk is necessary for the task**—we oftentimes put students into groups and then don't expect or want them to speak. We need to find the language in the curriculum and require students to speak while they are engaged in productive group worthy tasks. We just need to organize the talk so that students are talking about the right things.

3. **There is a clear outcome**—if we do not set an objective and organize the group work task, students will not be successful. Therefore, students need to know what the end goal should look like, by showing models and/or reviewing a rubric with clear expectations outlined.

4. **The task is cognitively appropriate**—students should not be completing simple tasks while in groups. Instead, tasks where students complete a deeper or more in-depth reading or experience with the content should be created. Students should need each other to complete these kinds of tasks, therefore tasks where an information gap is embedded in the group design are best.

5. **The task is integrated with a broader topic**—the group work task should assist, and not hinder, the progression and in-depth understanding of the content. Students should comprehend and internalize standards and objectives at a deeper level as a result of working with their peers, and being given another opportunity to explore content.

6. **All children are involved**—each student should have a specific role when they are involved in a group task. When students do not have specific roles, one or two students may end up completing the work for everyone else, which can cause resentment and frustration. Group structures, such as reciprocal teaching where each student has an accountable role assist with ensuring that all children are involved.

Continued

Figure 1.18 (Continued)

7. **Students have enough time**—when students have too much time, they can get off task and when they have too little time, they tend to get frustrated. It is important to approximate and gauge the average amount of time students need for a particular group task. Then, it is essential to monitor time by using a timer. If certain groups need more time and were on task, the teacher can make a decision about giving more time. There should also be a plan for differentiation, should some groups finish before others. I like to use bonus questions for groups that finish first, which requires anticipation and preplanning.

8. **Students know how to work in groups**—students will only know how to work in groups when each of the moves inside of the group are preplanned. That is, nothing should be left to chance. Each of the steps in the eight characteristics of productive group work should be practiced, some even independently, before expecting students to be successful with them in a smaller group setting.

Source: Adapted from Carstens (in Gibbons, 2002).

group worthy tasks. Teachers should have these points in front of them when planning for group work, in order to ensure that they are appropriately incorporated into lesson or unit development (a blank planning guide for group work is also available in the Appendix).

PLANNING GUIDE FOR PRODUCTIVE/EFFECTIVE GROUP WORK

✓ Clear and explicit instructions are provided.

- Lesson/unit incorporation: *article on global warming (informational text). I tell students that they are to reread the article that they previously read on global warming, only this time focusing in on one section, which they discuss with others using a Reciprocal Teaching role (summarizer, questioner, connector, or predictor; this approach is thoroughly discussed later in this chapter).*

✓ Talk is necessary for the task.

- *Students are required to discuss and teach their classmates the section of the article that they became an expert on using the Reciprocal Teaching role that they are assigned.*

✓ There is a clear outcome.

- *Students first reread the section of the article that they were given, also keeping in mind the specific role/focus that they were assigned to complete for their response (i.e., develop three questions about the text, or write three summary statements).*

✓ The task is cognitively appropriate.

  - *The global warming article is a grade-level text that adequately challenges students in comprehending and extending their knowledge of the content.*

✓ The task is integrated with the broader topic.

  - *The article on global warming lends itself to a second reading with a Reciprocal Teaching role because the text is quite dense and students can benefit from talking about the text in small groups.*

✓ All children are involved.

  - *Each student reads and becomes an expert on a section of the text that is reread with a particular role in mind, and then taught to classmates.*

✓ Students have enough time.

  - *Students have 10 minutes to reread their segment of the article on global warming, and 5 minutes to complete their assigned Reciprocal Teaching role. Once the 15 minutes are up, they have 5 to 10 minutes to discuss the reading selection in groups of four.*

✓ Students know how to work in groups.

  - *Prior to the assignment, the teacher has modeled and practiced each role within Reciprocal Teaching, before expecting students to complete the roles on their own and in groups.*

Source: Gibbons, 2002.

Notice how the Planning Guide for Productive/Effective Group Work assists a teacher with thinking through and anticipating the expectations for a group work project. Teachers can also build and plan for these eight characteristics during collaboration time so that group work is codeveloped and structured.

Connection to the CCSS
for Listening and Speaking Anchor Standard #1

An analysis of the College and Career Anchor Standard for Speaking and Listening #1 suggests: *Prepare for and participate effectively in a range of conversations and collaborations with diverse partners, building on others' ideas and expressing their own clearly and argumentatively.* Figure 1.19 is the progression of the Speaking and Listening Standards for Grades 7 through 10 for the College and Career Anchor Standard for Speaking and Listening

#1. The sections that are in bold are the manner in which this one standard builds from Grade 7 to Grade 10 so that educators might note the increasing expectations for Speaking and Listening for group work at the secondary level. The section that follows addresses how this standard progression may be explicitly taught in the classroom setting using the academic oral language development strategy of Reciprocal Teaching and Socratic Seminar.

Figure 1.19 Progression of the Speaking and Listening Standards for Grades 7 Through 10

Grade	Standards
7	1. Engage effectively in a range of collaborative discussions (one-on-one, in groups, and teacher-led) with diverse partners on **Grade 7 topics, texts, and issues**, building on others' ideas and expressing their own clearly. a. Come to discussion prepared, having read or researched material under study; explicitly draw on that preparation by referring to evidence on the topic, text, or issue to probe and reflect on ideas under discussion. b. Follow rules for collegial discussions, track progress toward specific goals and deadlines, and define individual roles as needed. c. Pose questions that elicit elaboration and respond to others' questions and comments with relevant observations and ideas that bring discussion back on topic as needed. d. Acknowledge new information expressed by others, and when warranted, modify their own views.
8	2. Engage effectively in a range of collaborative discussions (one-on-one, in groups, and teacher-led) with diverse partners on **Grade 8 topics, texts, and issues**, building on others' ideas and expressing their own clearly. a. Come to discussion prepared, having read or researched material under study; explicitly draw on that preparation by referring to evidence on the topic, text, or issue to probe and reflect on ideas under discussion. b. Follow rules for collegial discussions, track progress toward specific goals and deadlines, and define individual roles as needed. c. Pose questions that elicit elaboration and respond to others' questions and comments with relevant observations and ideas that bring discussion back on topic as needed. d. Acknowledge new information expressed by others, and when warranted, **qualify or justify their own views in light of the evidence presented**.

Grade	Standards
9–10	3. Engage effectively in a range of collaborative discussions (one-on-one, in groups, and teacher-led) with diverse partners on **Grades 9–10 topics, texts, and issues**, building on others' ideas and expressing their own clearly.
	a. Come to discussion prepared, having read or researched material under study; explicitly draw on that preparation **by referring to evidence from texts and other research on that topic or issue to stimulate a thoughtful, well-reasoned exchange of ideas.**
	b. **Work with peers to set rules for collegial discussion and decision making (e.g., informal consensus, taking votes on key issues, and presentation of alternate views), clear goals and deadlines, and individual roles as needed.**
	c. **Propel conversations by posing and responding to questions that relate the current discussion to broader themes or larger ideas; actively incorporate others into discussion; and clarify, verify, or challenge ideas and conclusions.**
	d. **Respond thoughtfully to diverse perspectives, summarize points of agreement and disagreement, and when warranted, qualify or justify their own views and understanding and make new connections in light of the evidence and reasoning presented.**

Source: NGA & CCSSO, 2010.

Progression of Listening and Speaking Anchor Standard #1 From Grades 7 to 8

The first progression in the Listening and Speaking Anchor Standard #1 from Grades 7 to 8 is that students must, "qualify or justify their own views in light of the evidence presented." This means that students need to read the text for a second or third time in order to find textual support for their thinking. This process scaffolds easily using Reciprocal Teaching and especially Socratic Seminar, which forces students to go back into the text to support their thoughts, in order to explain them to their group members.

The second progression seen in Grades 9 through 10 is similar, but adds a slightly more rigorous expectation for Listening and Speaking, which includes, "by referring to evidence from texts and other research on that topic or issue to stimulate a thoughtful, well-reasoned exchange of ideas." Notice, students are now expected to apply earlier expectations for Listening and Speaking in Grades 7 and 8, in other words their ideas must be justified with textual support, additionally the students must be prepared to substantiate "a thoughtful, well-reasoned exchange of ideas." Namely, they must know the information and text well enough that they can articulate the importance of their information with textual support for several rounds of discussion. This is notably more rigorous and the kind of academic conversations that are expected in the college setting.

Progression of Listening and Speaking Anchor Standard #1 From Grades 9 to 10

Additionally, the advancement in Listening and Speaking for Grades 9 through 10 includes the following progression (analysis of each progression is made immediately following each statement below):

Work with peers to set rules for collegial discussion and decision-making (e.g., informal consensus, taking votes on key issues, and presentation of alternate views), clear goals and deadlines, and individual roles as needed.

This listening and speaking substandard builds from earlier expectations in Grades K-2, where working with peers was explicitly expected and internalized. Now, however, the build in Grades 9–10 is that students need to make decisions, specifically coming to consensus, which was practiced earlier with Think-Pair-Share. Notice that there is also a democratic option for voting and taking into account multiple points of view. Lastly, this standard builds in expectations for the lifelong skills of monitoring oneself and holding group members accountable with goals, deadlines, and individual roles. The use of roles, goals, deadlines, and taking into account multiple points of view is explicitly taught using Reciprocal Teaching later in this section.

Propel conversations by posing and responding to questions that relate the current discussion to broader themes or larger ideas; actively incorporate others into discussion; and clarify, verify, or challenge ideas and conclusions.

The notion of questioning, clarifying, and connecting is explicitly practiced with Reciprocal Teaching, while challenging ideas and conclusions, as well as incorporating others into discussions is practiced with Socratic Seminar.

Respond thoughtfully to diverse perspectives, summarize points of agreement and disagreement, and when warranted, qualify or justify their own views and understanding and make new connections in light of the evidence and reasoning presented.

Opportunities for justifying one's thinking, as well as amending and building on another's views and ideas, using evidence, is explicitly taught, first with Reciprocal Teaching, which is a more structured approach to group work, and then using the Socratic Seminar method, which is less scaffolded.

The progression and build in Listening and Speaking Anchor Standard #1 for Grades 7 through 10 substantiates the need for apprenticing students into productive group work tasks, and then constantly embedding those standards into our teaching practices. The following section goes into greater detail around the elements of making group work successful in the classroom setting, beginning with building background knowledge and designing group worthy tasks.

GROUP WORK TO BUILD BACKGROUND KNOWLEDGE

Group work can be an essential part of building background knowledge for ELLs while they are in groups, as the role of building background knowledge is essential to language and content learning. It is important to acknowledge at the outset that ELLs *do* have background knowledge, but that it may not match mainstream American culture. In this way, schema is culturally specific, which is especially important to note with ELLs. Schema theory states that all knowledge is organized into units. When the meaning of the text or content is not part of a particular reader's cultural background, the schema can be skewed. Therefore, determining what students *do* know about a particular topic is an important place to begin so that we can build on those assets. This can be done with a variety of strategies, such as KWL charts (knows [K], wants to know [W], and has learned [L]), surveys, anticipation/reactions guides, or even posing questions on a Think-Pair-Share organizer regarding what students know about a topic so that they can expand on that knowledge base with their partner.

Ways to Build Background Knowledge

Once a teacher determines what students know and do not know about a topic, they can then begin planning ways to build background knowledge about new topics. Marzano (2004) suggests that building or activating background knowledge can be done either in direct or indirect ways. Below is a figure for teacher planning that illustrates direct and indirect ways of building background knowledge.

Direct ways of building background knowledge include hands-on and contextualized experiences, such as field trips, labs, guest speakers, and/ or simulations. Technology and online sources, such as Google Maps for

Figure 1.20 Building Background Knowledge

Direct Ways	Indirect Ways
• Lab experiment • Field trip • Hands-on activity • Guest speakers • Simulations	• Preplanned web searches • Series of pictures • Short video clips • Short reading selections on a topic

geography are indirect ways of building background knowledge. This type of online sources can also assist with the use of engaging tools that are relevant to students; however it is important to do some work and planning ahead of time with online sources so that students know which sources of information are reliable. Additional indirect ways to build background knowledge include showing a series of pictures or short video clips on a particular topic or theme. Teachers can also read a series of short reading selections—both informational and narrative—on the introduced theme or topic under study.

Selecting Group Worthy Tasks

Once a teacher selects a direct or indirect method of building background knowledge, they can plan an appropriate group worthy task to build up content knowledge. Group worthy tasks associated with building background knowledge around writing tasks at hand should be selected in order to assist students with strengthening content knowledge about a topic. In this way, group work helps promote language practice and can also be an engaging way to build background knowledge around topics to be written. Group structures like home/expert groups (e.g., where students become experts on certain content and then teach each other key information), is an effective way for ELLs to practice language and go in-depth about a topic. Home/expert groups create an information gap so that students need each other, and also need to practice academic oral language development in order to complete the group work tasks at hand.

One of the issues with writing is that students oftentimes do not have enough expertise to write about a particular topic, and therefore struggle with writing longer selections. Both project- and problem-based group work assist with this issue as well as ensure that more academic oral language development is used throughout the exercise, while also building content expertise. The following two group exchanges—Reciprocal

Teaching and Socratic Seminar—are ways to structure productive group work in advance so that students can become skilled at more sophisticated group work structures.

Small Group Exchanges: Reciprocal Teaching Strategy

Reciprocal teaching refers to an instructional activity that takes place in the form of a dialogue between teachers and students regarding segments of text. The dialogue is structured by the use of four comprehension strategies: *summarizing, question generating, clarifying, and predicting.* The teacher and students take turns assuming the role of teacher in leading this dialogue. The purpose of reciprocal teaching is to facilitate a group effort between and among teacher and students to bring meaning to the text.

Reading researchers Brown and Palincsar (1985) selected each of the reciprocal teaching strategies as a "means of aiding students to construct meaning from text, as well as a means of monitoring their reading to ensure that they are in fact understanding what they read" (p. 66). This strategy, then, can be used in a productive group work setting to assign each student an accountable role for academic talk (by assuming one of the four reading tasks—summarizing, questioning, clarifying, or predicting), while also reinforcing good reader habits with ELLs.

Figure 1.21   Why Reciprocal Teaching?

- **Definition:** Reciprocal teaching refers to an instructional activity that takes place in the form of a **dialogue** **between teachers and students regarding segments of text**. The dialogue is structured by the use of four comprehension strategies: **summarizing, question generating, clarifying, and predicting.** The teacher and students **take turns** assuming the role of teacher in leading this dialogue.

Figure 1.22   Reciprocal Teaching

- **Purpose:** The purpose of reciprocal teaching is to **facilitate a group effort** between teacher and students, as well as among students, in the task of **bringing meaning to the text**.
- Reading researchers Palincsar and Brown (1985) selected each of the reciprocal teaching strategies as a means of aiding students to **construct meaning** from text, as well as a means of **monitoring their reading** to ensure that they are in fact **understanding what they read**.

Reciprocal Teaching Steps

After the first reading of a text, each student engages specifically with the selection a second time by either summarizing what they read; creating questions for discussion about the text; predicting what might happen next using textual evidence; or clarifying or connecting the text to another text, life, or society. Because there are four reciprocal reading roles, students can be placed in home groups of four to complete their specific role—either summarizing, questioning, clarifying, or predicting. ELLs can also use academic language stems associated with their specific role (i.e., "The most important portion of the text was on page ____, because . . .") to begin a discussion about their findings from the text. Requiring students to cite and go back into the text to substantiate their thoughts reinforces expectations within the CCSS. This style of small group conversations also apprentice students into building on each other's ideas so that they continue that practice later with a whole or larger group academic conversation.

Additional Reciprocal Teaching Support

In order to build another layer of support with the reciprocal teaching strategy, students with similar roles from each smaller group can work together. For example, all of the summarizers can meet in one group, all of the questioners in another group, and so on. These groups are called expert groups by role and the students can then come to consensus about their ideas before sharing out with their respective home

Figure 1.23 Reciprocal Teaching Roles

A. **Summarizer:** What are the **three most important** events/details from the reading and explain why they are important and how they are connected?

B. **Questioner:** Pose **at least three questions** about the text—these questions could address confusing parts of the text or thoughts you wonder about.

C. **Predictor:** Identify **at least three** text-related predictions—these predictions should help the group anticipate what will happen next.

D. **Connector:** Make **at least three** connections between the reading and your own experience, the world, or another piece of text.

groups. Students, including ELLs, should be homogeneously grouped in their home groups so that there are language models within each group. These group roles should also switch with each reading selection so that there are a variety of opportunities for students to master each of the roles. Lastly, before expecting students to complete these roles successfully on their own and in groups, teachers should model and complete each role as a whole group several times. Group conversations and norms should similarly be modeled several times so that true collaboration ensues in individual groups. A blank graphic organizer and role cards are included in the Appendix for use during productive group work time.

A Reciprocal Teaching Classroom Conversation

The following is a reciprocal teaching conversation that could occur after students read a text about microorganisms during a science lesson. During this conversation, the students read the entire text as a whole class first, and then for a second reading, each student goes deeper into the reading selection by discussing their individual role, either summarizing, questioning, predicting, or connecting. Students are held accountable for the conversation by how carefully they listen to each other, how well they clarify their responses, and then summarize what they heard each group member say by writing it in the appropriate graphic organizer section.

Notice in Figure 1.25 how students are able to further internalize and go deeper around the concept of microorganisms because they are using the four key comprehension skills of summarizing, questioning, predicting, and connecting. After students share their ideas in small groups, the teacher should then select students to share their ideas with the entire class.

Accountable Talk: Using the Power Walk

As students discuss in groups, the teacher should walk around the room monitoring student conversations and listening for students who might share out with the entire group. This is called the power walk and demonstrates to students that there are layers of accountability for academic talk. This is also a time for the teacher to monitor conversations that might have gone off task. Students typically feel validated when asked to share out their responses. Additionally, teachers should strategically select student responses that make the conversation richer and take the conversation

Figure 1.24 Reciprocal Teaching Graphic Organizer

Summarizing	Questioning	Predicting	Connecting
Beyond retelling what happens in the reading, identify what you think are the *three most important events/details* from the reading and explain why they are important and how they are connected.	Pose at least *three questions about the reading*; these could include questions that address confusing parts of the reading, or thought questions that the reading makes you wonder about.	Identify at least *three text-related predictions*; these predictions should be based on new developments in the reading and your predictions should help the group to anticipate what happens next.	Make at least *three connections between ideas or events* in the reading to your own experience, the world around you, or other texts. Be prepared to explain these connections to your group.

Figure 1.25 Reciprocal Teaching Graphic Organizer

Summarizing	Questioning	Predicting	Connecting
Beyond retelling what happens in the reading, identify what you think are the *three most important events/details* from the reading and explain why they are important and how they are connected.	Pose at least *three questions about the reading*; these could include questions that address confusing parts of the reading, or thought questions that the reading makes you wonder about.	Identify at least *three text-related predictions*; these predictions should be based on new developments in the reading and your predictions should help the group to anticipate what will happen next.	Make at least *three connections between ideas or events* in the reading to your own experience, the world around you, or other texts. Be prepared to explain these connections to your group.
Microorganisms are really small and can't be seen with the eye.	*What are microorganisms and why are they important?*	*Using the words in bold, titles and pictures, what do you think this selection will be about?*	*I connect this to the movie "Outbreak" where there were germs all over the place, but they weren't good for those humans.*
Microorganisms are everywhere, including our clothes and body.	*What would happen without microorganisms?*	*I see a microscope and the word microorganism used throughout, so I think that microorganisms are really small.*	*I remember when we read about how some germs can be good for us.* *My mom says to not use antibacterial soap too much because we need some bacteria.*
Microorganisms aren't bad. We need a certain amount of them.	*Are we going to be able to look at microorganisms under a microscope?*		

deeper. Lastly, by having one student from each role share out with the whole group, we are embedding message redundancy and message quantity, where students hear the message several times and from several different sources.

REMOVING THE SCAFFOLD: RECIPROCAL TEACHING IN A HIGH SCHOOL ENGLISH CLASS

The pictures in Figure 1.26 are Reciprocal Teaching artifacts from a tenth grade classroom in the Los Angeles area. The students in this class were reading *The Stranger* by Albert Camus in Reciprocal Teaching groups, and had internalized the process to such an extent, that they began to add steps to the process. Because the Reciprocal Teaching graphic organizer is intended as a scaffold that is eventually eliminated, this example shows that midway through the school year students (including ELLs) were able to move above and beyond the four steps in the handout.

The picture on the left details the additional steps that students in this tenth grade class decided that they wanted to add to their reciprocal teaching time. The students determined that they wanted to begin with making predictions each time, as they felt that this skill best prepared them to read the next section. The next skill they wanted to adopt was questioning and

Figure 1.26   South El Monte High School: 10th Grade ELA

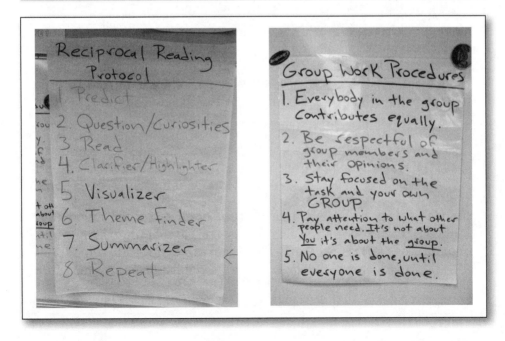

then added the notion of curiosities, as they felt it assisted them with pre-paring to read. They also chose that after reading a section of the text, with the number of pages predetermined by the group (after the teacher prede-termined the number of pages for the first semester), they agreed that they wanted to take a vocabulary pause for 1 to 2 minutes. The class believed that this was important because they saw that as they read several pages, they typically had questions about key words that they might not under-stand. Students had discussions as a group about words that they did not understand, and then used resources like a vocabulary log, for words that were still not clear to them from the group conversation.

Vocabulary clarification was included as a part of the overall clarifica-tion along with highlighting key or confusing portions of the text. The students wanted visualizing and connecting which are similar processes to follow next. They felt that as they visualized key components of the text, they could make personal and text-based connections. The theme finder was also a step that the class determined was important, as they wanted to track how themes were developing from section to section,

Figure 1.27 Group Work Procedures

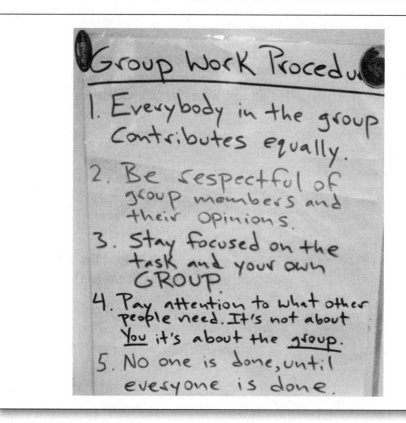

until a final summary was constructed from the conversation. Notice that students then determined that before they started the cycle all over again, they needed to pay special attention to evaluating the protagonist (Meursault, in this particular book selection) in order to better understand his character.

Figure 1.27 represents the group work norms and procedures that the class selected as points of consensus during reciprocal teaching time. Notice how these five procedures embody the CCSS Anchor Standard for Speaking and Listening in Grades 9–10. This standard (#1b) states that students are expected to "work with peers to set rules for collegial discussions and decision-making (e.g., informal consensus, taking votes on key issues, presentation of alternate views), clear goals and deadlines, and individual roles as needed" (CCSS, 2013). Many of the other components of Standard #1 are also embodied through the implementation of reciprocal teaching in this high school classroom, but group work can only really be productive when students have a voice in determining the agreed upon norms and procedures.

Whole Group Exchanges: Socratic Seminar Strategy

Socratic seminar also directly connects to Key CCSS ELA Practice 5, the Speaking and Listening standards, which require students to "Participate in purposeful collaborative conversations with partners as well as in small and large groups" (CCSS, 2013). In particular, as students become proficient and comfortable with reciprocal teaching discussions in small groups, whole class, or large group discussions, then using the Socratic seminar method that involves less structured discussions can be used. Socratic seminars are based on the teachings of Socrates who believed in the power of asking questions, inquiry over memorizing information, and dialogue instead of debate. Socratic seminars also connect to the teachings of Vygotsky, Piaget, Dewey, and Friere, who all believed that learning was a social process. Israel (2002) succinctly defines Socratic seminars and describes their importance for students:

> The Socratic seminar is a formal discussion, based on a text, in which the leader asks open-ended questions. Within the context of the discussion, students listen closely to the comments of others, thinking critically for themselves, and articulate their own thoughts and their responses to the thoughts of others. They learn to work cooperatively and to question intelligently and civilly. (p. 89)

As suggested in the description above, Socratic seminar discussions typically begin with an open-ended question that is posed by the teacher or a student. Students examine the text independently to obtain and substantiate their answers, which requires a second reading exposure. Once students have identified their ample evidence, an academic discussion can occur. The fishbowl method (where half of the class sits on the inside of a circle, while the other half sits outside of the circle) promotes careful listening in a Socratic seminar discussion when half of the class participates in discussing one segment while others listen. In a second discussion, groups switch the discussing and listening roles.

Teacher and Student Roles During Socratic Seminar

The following section describes both the teacher and student's role during Socratic seminar discussions. Although teachers take on more of a facilitative role during Socratic seminar, they can play a more active role in the beginning by determining the open-ended questions that connect to the text, which are posed to the group. Eventually, students take over this planning, just as is the expectation with the Listening and Speaking Anchor Standard #1 in the upper grades. The teacher's role then progresses to monitor to ensure that conversations are on target and that students are justifying their thinking and responses by using textual evidence.

Student accountability to group norms and discussion preparation is essential to the success of Socratic seminar. In particular, students have to read the text carefully enough to be able to justify their thinking (notice here specific connections to Listening and Speaking Anchor Standard #1). Additionally, students should understand that they are having an academic conversation and not a debate. The guidelines for Socratic seminar use are included in Figures 1.28 and 1.29 and also found in the Appendix.

Procedures for Socratic Seminar

When students first start working on Socratic seminar, it is helpful to review the following two procedures: 1) Respond to the seminar's opening question; and 2) Examine the reading selection to support your answer. These procedures ensure that students are accountable to the Socratic seminar process, dialogue, and each other. As noted previously, the seminar's opening question should be open-ended, because this type of question requires more dialogue and critical thinking processes. By giving students ample time to consider the questions in advance, they can examine the text carefully to support their responses. Students can also use the academic language stems to begin Socratic seminar conversations. This method also assists them with learning the important skill of how to disagree with each other politely.

Figure 1.28   Socratic Seminar: A Structure for Classroom Talk

Procedures for Socratic Seminar
- Respond to the seminar's opening question.
- Examine the reading selection to support your answer.

Academic Language Stems
- *I agree with . . . but would like to add . . .*
- *I disagree with . . . because*
- *I need clarification on . . .*
- *I am confused by . . .*

Guidelines for Socratic Seminar

Just as it is true with Think-Pair-Share and Reciprocal Teaching, it is important for students to listen carefully to each other during Socratic seminar sessions. There are three guidelines for Socratic seminar which include: 1) Listen carefully; 2) Participate openly; and 3) Value others' opinions, but refer to the reading selection to defend your position. Each of the three guidelines are explained below.

Remember that if these three active listening skills are thoroughly practiced with the two other academic oral language and active listening strategies (Think-Pair-Share and Reciprocal teaching), then they are more likely to occur with Socratic seminar, because it is less structured. Nevertheless, in order to listen openly students should be reminded to face classmates when they are sharing, and not to merely listen for a response, but to fully comprehend their colleagues' points of view and perspectives.

Open participation means that students must come to class prepared with a profound reading of the text so that they are confident enough with their responses and can exchange ideas. They have to produce ample evidence of their ideas from the text, so they need to be taught how to annotate a text, including highlighting and adding their own thoughts to a

Figure 1.29   Guidelines and Procedures for Socratic Seminar

Guidelines for Socratic Seminar
- Listen carefully.
- Participate openly.
- Value others' opinions, but refer to the reading selection to defend your position.

particular quote or portion of a text. Since students have practiced summarizing a partner's response via Think-Pair-Share and summarizing the most important portions of a text with Reciprocal teaching, they should not find this lesson too difficult to complete. ELLs may need additional support in how to expand and/or clarify their ideas, so after teacher modeling, students can work in partners and/or small groups to practice this skill before the actual Socratic seminar session.

By using academic language stems, such as "I understand where you're coming from, but I disagree because . . ." or "I agree with you, but would like to add . . . ," the students are taught how to validate and value each other's responses, even when they disagree. Additionally, students should also be explicitly taught that using such polite and respectful language opens up a conversation, and in this way, how Socratic seminar differs from a debate, where sides are taken.

The beginning of a Socratic seminar conversation might begin something like the one in Figure 1.30.

Notice here how the teacher can interject and assist students with going deeper into the text. In this way, teachers should monitor Socratic seminar conversations closely and find ways that students can push each other's thinking. As ELLs become more comfortable with Socratic seminar, they are able to expand their thought process. Similar academic conversations can begin as early as the fourth grade, as the displayed Anchor Standard #1 for Listening and Speaking begins to make some of these expectations clear.

Figure 1.30 Example of a Socratic Seminar Conversation

Teacher	ELL 1	ELL 2
What portion of the text resonated for you the most?	The section where Ramiro explains to Luis that he is joining a gang is most important to me because the two are finally communicating with each other, and trying to understand one another.	I agree with Jonathan, and would like to add that this section is most important because Luis finally tells Ramiro openly that he fears that he will follow in his footsteps. They are finally honest with each other.
Let's go to page 25 in the text and find evidence for how this becomes a turning point for the two in their relationship.		

Figure 1.31 CCSS for Listening and Speaking, Grade 4

Grade 4 Students: Engage effectively in a range of collaborative discussions (one-on-one, in groups, and teacher-led) with diverse partners on Grade 4 topics and texts, building on others' ideas and expressing their own clearly.

a. Come to discussions prepared, having read or studied required material; explicitly drawing on that preparation and other information known about the topic to explore ideas under discussion.
b. Follow agreed-upon rules for discussion and carry out assigned roles.
c. Pose and respond to specific questions to clarify or follow up on information, and make comments that contribute to the discussion and link the remarks of others.
d. Review the key ideas expressed and explain their own ideas and understanding in light of the discussion.

2 Moving From Speaking to Writing Across Genres (the Curriculum Cycle)

There are four literacy domains: listening, speaking, reading, writing. Since writing is the most cognitively and linguistically demanding of the four domains, unpacking the organizational structures of each type of writing unveils what is often the hidden curriculum of school for many students. Unfortunately, as educators, we oftentimes do not take the time to explicitly teach students the insides of each kind of writing genre. Many times, we assume that students will naturally pick up these expectations when reading, or as we provide model/benchmark papers. It is only with this kind of explicit teaching and modeling, however, that many students, especially ELLs, are able to function successfully as capable and proficient writers. It is these kinds of skills that students take with them to college and beyond, where writing demands also vary from field to field and from discipline to discipline.

The writing demands of the Common Core State Standards (CCSS) further require educators to become more explicit and intentional about writing expectations. Three writing genres in particular are identified—narrative, informational, and argumentative—which sanctions educators to intensely focus on allowing students, especially ELLs, to achieve success with these genres over time.

Since the distribution of emphasis is on the three genres of writing—narrative, informational, and argumentative—teachers can be more efficient in their plans for writing instruction. For example, in contrast to prior standards movements, there is less of an emphasis on short, focused research projects. Additionally, since the narrative writing genre has been given less importance, it is essential to distribute time to each genre according to emphasis. There is also a shift in the expectations for narrative writing, which are now more evidence-based. This does not mean that we should not teach to the narrative genre, but instead that we really need to examine the specific expectations for each genre in order that our students are adequately prepared and successful. In this way, it is important to note that these shifts in emphasis on instruction come from the desire to prepare ELLs for college and career, as well as 21st century expectations, where narrative writing might not be emphasized as greatly.

Figure 2.1 is a chart of the writing expectations called out by the CCSS. The first three items highlighted speak to the characteristics of each of the genres of writing.

Figure 2.1 Chart of Writing Expectations

Writing
1. Write arguments to support claims in an analysis of substantive topics or texts, using valid reasoning and relevant and sufficient evidence.
2. Write informative/explanatory texts to examine and convey complex ideas and information clearly and accurately through the effective selection, organization, and analysis of content.
3. Write narratives to develop real or imagined experiences or events using effective technique, well-chosen details, and well-structured event sequences.
4. Produce clear and coherent writing in which the development, organization, and style are appropriate to task, purpose, and audience.
5. Develop and strengthen writing by planning, revising, editing, rewriting, or trying a new approach.
6. Use technology, including the Internet, to produce and publish writing and to interact and collaborate with others.
7. Conduct short as well as more sustained research projects based on focused questions, demonstrating understanding of the subject under investigation.

Writing
8. Gather relevant information from multiple print and digital sources, assess the credibility and accuracy of each source, and integrate the information while avoiding plagiarism.
9. Draw evidence from literary or informational texts to support analysis, reflection, and research.
10. Write routinely over extended time frames (time for research, reflection, and revision) and shorter time frames (a single sitting or a day or two) for a range of tasks, purposes, and audiences.

Source: NGA & CCSSO, 2010.

Notice that the additional expectations for writing have been laid out in the chart above (#5–10). Although these areas are not addressed specifically in this section, they are referred to in varying degrees by the scaffolding suggested in the writing framework below.

INTEGRATION OF LANGUAGE WITH CONTENT

One of the major shifts within the CCSS is the integration of language across content areas. Developed by Stanford University's Understanding Language (2012), the Venn diagram in Figure 2.2 visually demonstrates how language is at the center of each of the content area standards expectations.

In the middle, we see that the language overlap for all three content areas—Math, Science, and English Language Arts—include:

- E2. Build a strong base of knowledge through content rich texts—students need to be exposed to a variety of texts and sources, both expository and narrative in order to thoroughly write about a topic across content areas;
- E5. Read, write, and speak grounded in evidence—students need to be taught how to make evidence-based claims, which is an important shift from personal opinions or feeling-based writing tasks that they might be used to;
- M3 and E4. Construct viable arguments and critique reasoning of others—building on the notion of evidence-based claims, students need to know how to construct logical and sound arguments that can be well supported by evidence; and
- S7. Engage in argument from evidence—students need to be taught how to engage in academic discourse and writing that is grounded in solid evidence from reliable sources.

As educators, knowing and understanding the areas of language that overlap among the content areas prove to be an important support system

Figure 2.2 Relationships and Convergences

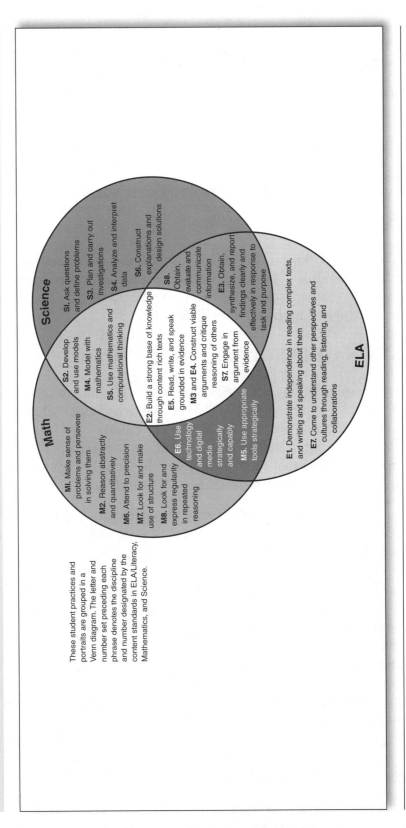

These student practices and portraits are grouped in a Venn diagram. The letter and number set preceding each phrase denotes the discipline and number designated by the content standards in ELA/Literacy, Mathematics, and Science.

Math

M1. Make sense of problems and persevere in solving them

M2. Reason abstractly and quantitatively

M6. Attend to precision

M7. Look for and make use of structure

M8. Look for and express regularly in repeated reasoning

Science

S1. Ask questions and define problems

S3. Plan and carry out investigations

S4. Analyze and interpret data

S6. Construct explanations and design solutions

S2. Develop and use models

M4. Model with mathematics

S5. Use mathematics and computational thinking

E6. Use technology and digital media strategically and capably

M5. Use appropriate tools strategically

E2. Build a strong base of knowledge through content rich texts

E5. Read, write, and speak grounded in evidence

M3 and **E4.** Construct viable arguments and critique reasoning of others

S7. Engage in argument from evidence

S8. Obtain, evaluate and communicate information

E3. Obtain, synthesize, and report findings clearly and effectively in response to task and purpose

ELA

E1. Demonstrate independence in reading complex texts, and writing and speaking about them

E7. Come to understand other perspectives and cultures through reading, listening, and collaborations

Sources:

Achieve, 2013, pp. 41–82 (Science and Engineering Practices).

NGA & CCSSO, 2010b, p. 7 (Student Portraits).

NGA & CCSSO, 2010c, pp. 6–8 (Practices).

Understanding Language Initiative, 2012.

for ELLs, especially as they acquire language and learn to function within the rigorous demands of the CCSS. The lessons developed in this section require ELLs to engage in the overlap practices suggested above within three content areas, including English Language Arts, History/Social Studies, and Science.

In the next section, a framework and organizational structure for how to address each of the three genres of writing is described, with an incorporation of language development at the center. This incorporation goes a long way in meeting the specific language needs of ELLs when approaching written tasks. The framework presents a process for explicitly teaching the writing "development, organization, and style . . . appropriate to task, purpose, and audience" using a strategic lesson plan template (CCSS, 2013). This section also incorporates and ties together the academic language development (ALD) strategies from Chapter 1 as scaffolds for moving from speaking to writing.

The Curriculum Cycle

One method of explicitly teaching each genre of writing is called the Curriculum Cycle, developed by Pauline Gibbons in 2002. This system allows students, especially ELLs, to organize each new genre of writing by explicitly teaching the structure of each new style of writing introduced. As Gibbons (2002) suggests, "ELLs are less likely to be familiar with the particular organizational structure of different kinds of writing, and with the grammatical structure of English" (p. 58). Since basic grammatical structures in English are new to ELLs, and are oftentimes taught in rote and meaningless ways, contextualizing those structures within each genre of writing proves helpful to ELLs, as they progress as writers.

Figure 2.3 is a beneficial tool that describes each of the five most common writing genres that students encounter in school, with a specific focus on the three genres called out in the CCSS—narrative, argumentative, and informational genres. In the first row, the specific text type is noted, along with a suggested prompt. In the second row, the purpose of each writing style is described. The third row includes the particular organizational structure that is expected for each writing genre. In the fourth row, the connectives or linking verbs associated with the writing style are included. Lastly, the fifth row includes additional language features that are associated with this genre of writing. The highlighted columns are the specific genres that are addressed in this section of the book, including a lesson plan guide written around the Curriculum Cycle format.

The Curriculum Cycle Features chart can be used whenever a new writing genre is introduced. The elements of writing should be explicitly

Figure 2.3 Curriculum Cycle Features

Type of Text	Recount	Narrative (story)	Report	Procedure/Informational	Discussion (one side) Argument
	What I did at the weekend?	The Elephant and the Mouse CCSS=20 percent	Insects	How to make a healthy meal CCSS=40 percent	(two sides) (e.g., should smoking be made illegal?) CCSS=40 percent
Purpose	To tell what happened	To entertain, to teach	To give information	To tell how to do something	To persuade others, to take a position and justify it.
Organization	• Orientation (tells who, where, when) • Series of events • Personal comment/conclusion	• Orientation (tells who, where, when) • Series of events • Problem • Resolution	• General statement • Characteristics (e.g., habitat) • Characteristics (e.g., appearance) • Characteristics (e.g., food, etc.) • May have subheadings	• Goal • Steps in sequence	• Personal statement of position • Argument(s) and supporting evidence • Possibly counter-argument(s) and supporting evidence • Conclusion
Connectives (Linking Words)	To do with time (first, then, next, afterwards, at the end of the day)	To do with time (first, then, next, afterwards, at the end of the day)	Not usually used	First, second, third, finally, etc.	First, second, in addition, therefore, however, on the other hand
Other Language Features	Past tense, tells about what happened • Describing words	Past tense, tells about what happened • Action verbs • May have dialogue and verbs of "saying"	Uses "to be" and "to have" (e.g., A fly is an insect. It has six legs.) • Special vocabulary	Uses verbs to give instructions (e.g., take, mix, add, chop, bake, etc.)	May use argumentative language (e.g., it is obviously wrong)

Source: Adapted from Gibbons, 2002.

taught each time a new genre of writing is introduced. The specific portion of the chart that is taught should be posted in the room so that it becomes a reference point for students. The chart is not meant to be inclusive of all writing genres, and depending on text types being introduced, the chart can be augmented. Mentor texts and joint construction of writing can also be used along with this chart.

The Curriculum Cycle also connects to Key CCSS ELA Practice 2: *Produce clear and coherent writing in which the development, organization, and style are appropriate to task, purpose, and audience* (CCSS, 2013). For each new writing genre that is expected of ELLs, the following cycle is introduced:

- **A specific purpose for writing**—explicitly stating the purpose and reason for the writing assignment; connecting the writing to real-world application (e.g., scientists and historians write in this style).
- **A particular overall structure for writing**—providing a clear description of the organization of the writing genre. If there is an organizational pattern, making that clear to students (e.g., for argumentation, presenting an argument and anticipating/addressing counterarguments).
- **Connectives**—introducing the specific transition words associated with the particular writing genre (e.g., for procedural writing, the use of enumeration).
- **Specific linguistic features**—providing students with the grammatical tense that they should be writing in, as well the specialized vocabulary associated with the writing style (e.g., narrative writing selections can include dialogue).

A GENRE APPROACH TO TEACHING WRITING

Advancements in both the 21st century and in college and career requirements dictate that students not only need to read and speak effectively, they also need to know how to function within each genre of writing as they move from discipline to discipline, and assignment to assignment. In this section, three of the more common writing genres are unpacked using the Curriculum Cycle. In Chapter 3, the narrative writing genre is introduced in English/Language Arts; in Chapter 4, argumentative writing is introduced in History/Social Studies; and in Chapter 5, informational/expository writing is addressed in Science.

Each of these writing lessons adheres to the following design: building background knowledge; addressing the academic oral language and specialized vocabulary around the topic within the discipline; and explicitly teaching the specific discipline's genre of writing associated with the Curriculum

Cycle. For each chapter, a lesson plan organizer for the writing genre is provided (see Figure 2.4). As teachers begin to build their own lesson plans using this framework, I encourage them to use this organizer as a guide to address and scaffold the language expectations of the CCSS. Examples of how to use the lesson plan organizer follow each of the writing genre chapters.

Key Elements of the Curriculum Cycle Lesson Plan

In addition to the Curriculum Cycle portion of the lesson plan, there are three other sections (which appear at the beginning of the lesson plan guide) that assist with important content and language scaffolds for ELLs, as noted and explained below. The remainder of the lesson plan organizer elements follow this sequence.

First, there is a section and time devoted to building background knowledge around the writing topic selected using hands-on and contextualized experiences. This is essential because if students do not have ample background knowledge regarding a topic, they are not able to write in depth about it.

Target vocabulary is also explicitly taught using the Frayer model, and is connected to the building background knowledge experience (Frayer, 1969). If students do not have an ample and descriptive vocabulary set, their writing is stale and uninteresting. Many ELLs come to school with a listening vocabulary of far fewer words—1,000 words versus 5,000 to 7,000

Figure 2.4   Curriculum Cycle Lesson Plan Organizer

Common Core State Standard	
Writing Objective	
Building Background Knowledge for Content of Writing	
Specialized Vocabulary Needed (Frayer, 1969)	
Academic Oral Language Development (Think-Pair-Share With Open-ended Questions)	
Purpose	
Organization	
Connectives	
Other Linguistic Features	

Source: Soto, 2012.

Figure 2.5 Key Elements of the Curriculum Cycle Lesson Plan

Building Background Knowledge for Writing Topic/Genre	
Specialized Vocabulary Needed (Frayer model)	
Academic Oral Language Development (Think-Pair-Share With Open-ended Questions)	

Source: Soto, 2012.

words for native English speakers (Soto-Hinman & Hetzel, 2009). This linguistic gap is one of the first that ELLs must overcome in order to be able to acquire English fluently, as well as function academically, both in oral and written language.

Lastly, as suggested in Chapter 1 of this book, open-ended questions need to be constructed for academic oral language development using Think-Pair-Share. This is a strategy that scaffolds speaking and listening experiences for ELLs so that they can move from speaking to writing effectively, and in a more expansive manner. Each of the sections offer in-depth explanations of these three elements of the lesson design.

Transferring Background Knowledge Into Writing Success

The building background knowledge section of the lesson plan is essential for ELLs so that they have enough vocabulary and content knowledge to write about the topic at hand. Ensuring that students know enough about what they are writing about in order to extensively cover a subject is one of the most essential components of any writing lesson. Additionally, although ELLs frequently have background knowledge regarding their own home countries and culture, they may not have background knowledge associated with mainstream American culture, or the selected topic. Consequently, they need those experiences to close the background experience gap and have something concrete to write about the topic (Soto-Hinman & Hetzel, 2009). Each lesson developed using this tutorial design begins with a hands-on experience where students gain ample background knowledge associated with the writing content and purpose. Figure 2.6 lists several idea starters for building background knowledge with students, including hands-on and contextualized experiences from Soto-Hinman and Hetzel's 2009 book, *Literacy Gaps*.

Figure 2.6 Gap Between the Student and the Text

STUDENT	GAP	TEXT
	Background knowledge and experience	
	Bridge Building Strategies	
	Field Trips	
	Simulations	
	Video Clips	
	Total Physical Response	
	Demonstrations	
	Guest Speakers	
	K-W-L Charts	
	Anticipation Guides	
	Vocabulary Knowledge Self-Assessment	

Source: Soto-Hinman & Hetzel, 2009.

The figure shows that the gap between the student and the text often results in a lack of background knowledge. The strategies in the center are ones that teachers can utilize in order to build schema around the writing topic. For example, teachers can take students on field trips or create simulations of historical or literary events. Similarly, teachers can show brief videos about the topic or introduced content as well as having students act out scenes or watch science or math demonstrations with active listening exercises embedded. When they are planning lessons utilizing the Curriculum Cycle, teachers should carefully think through how they provide ample, interactive, and accessible input from ELLs.

Incorporating the Frayer Model Into the Lesson Plan Organizer

Once students are exposed to adequate background knowledge building experiences, key vocabulary is introduced using the Frayer model. Introducing key vocabulary after the hands-on and contextualized experiences allows students to have enough familiarity with the concept to attach the specific linguistic vocabulary label. As suggested in the CCSS language chart (Figure 2.7), students, including ELLs, need to be able to "determine or clarify the meaning of unknown and multiple-meaning words . . ." as well as "demonstrate an understanding of word relationships and nuances in word meanings" (CCSS, 2013). The Frayer model allows educators to scaffold expectations for students by explicitly teaching words that students may not understand. Since speaking and application of language is essential, students are also expected to "acquire and use accurately a range of general and academic domain-specific words and phrases sufficiently in reading, writing, speaking, and listening" (CCSS, 2013). Only through explicit teaching and multiple exposures to new words can ELLs internalize and apply new word knowledge in all domains.

The Frayer model approach allows students to begin to do the word work expected of them in order to communicate academically in both spoken and written language. Figure 2.8 is a blank Frayer model template and a description of how to use the strategy follows below it.

The Frayer model strategy is not intended to be an independent activity and should be completed with the whole class. Teachers should select five to seven key words from the unit that they plan to use with the vocabulary development strategy. The power of this strategy lies in the many examples that are generated in conjunction with the target word, thus closing the vocabulary gap quickly and efficiently. Figure 2.9 illustrates a chart emphasizing Beck, McKeown, and Kucan's (2002) work on the Tiered Approach to vocabulary instruction. Because this model strategy takes time to do well, only Tier II (high utility—across content areas or contexts) and Tier III (abstract/nuanced—found only in that selection) words should be used with this strategy (Beck, McKeown, & Kucan, 2002).

Notice that Tier I words are basic words for which ELLs may understand the concept, but not the linguistic label. These words are more commonly taught in English Language Development courses. Tier II and Tier

Figure 2.7   CCSS Language Chart

1. Demonstrate command of the conventions of standard English grammar and usage.
2. Demonstrate conventions of standard English capitalization, punctuation, and spelling when writing.
3. Understand language to apply in different contexts, make effective choices for meaning or style, and comprehend more fully when reading or listening.
4. Determine or clarify the meaning of unknown and multiple connotation words and phrases by using context clues, analyzing meaningful word parts.
5. Demonstrate understanding of word relationships and nuances in word meanings.
6. Acquire and accurately use a range of general academic and domain-specific words and phrases appropriate for reading, writing, speaking, and listening.

Source: NGA & CCSSO, 2010.

Figure 2.8 Frayer Model Organizer

DEFINITION	VISUAL/PICTURE
EXAMPLES/MODELS Target Word:	NON-EXAMPLES

Source: Frayer, 1969.

III words are typically taught in content area classrooms, with Tier II words oftentimes extending across content areas, and Tier III words frequently specific to a context or discipline.

Scaffolding the Frayer Model

Once students have adequate background knowledge around a word, the teacher begins in the Frayer model template (Figure 2.8) on the bottom left hand corner, eliciting examples from students so that the graphic organizer is completed together. Students can also partner talk with each other to determine examples of the target word first, which can then be shared with the whole group and confirmed before moving on to non-examples.

Secondly, students are asked to determine non-examples found on the bottom right hand corner of the template. These should not just be the opposite of the examples nor random words, such as hot dog or animal.

Figure 2.9 Which Words to Teach?

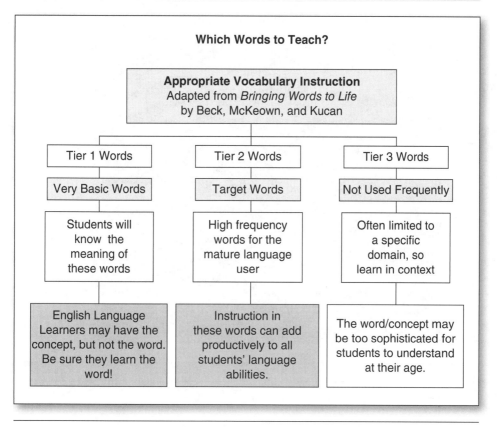

Which Words to Teach?

Appropriate Vocabulary Instruction
Adapted from *Bringing Words to Life*
by Beck, McKeown, and Kucan

Tier 1 Words	Tier 2 Words	Tier 3 Words
Very Basic Words	Target Words	Not Used Frequently
Students will know the meaning of these words	High frequency words for the mature language user	Often limited to a specific domain, so learn in context
English Language Learners may have the concept, but not the word. Be sure they learn the word!	Instruction in these words can add productively to all students' language abilities.	The word/concept may be too sophisticated for students to understand at their age.

Source: Beck, McKeown, & Kucan, 2002.

Instead, the non-examples are words that are in close proximity to the overall concept and target word identified. The third step is developing a visual (upper right corner) that is a personal representation and/or memory of the target word that assists students to remember the word.

Finally, the class together constructs and comes to consensus regarding a definition of the word by filling in the upper left hand corner, using both examples and the visual representation as a guide. I prefer that students use at least two ideas from the examples section in their final definition. Additionally, students can create their own definitions, or work with a partner to come to consensus around a definition. When this strategy is first taught to students, teachers should request a class definition from the students. Eventually, students can keep their own definitions and also work with the teacher to come up with a class definition. As the unit progresses, background knowledge around the word further evolves and deepens so that students can add to the examples and refine the final definition. Figure 2.10 is a student example of a Frayer model.

Figure 2.10 Frayer Model: Dawdled

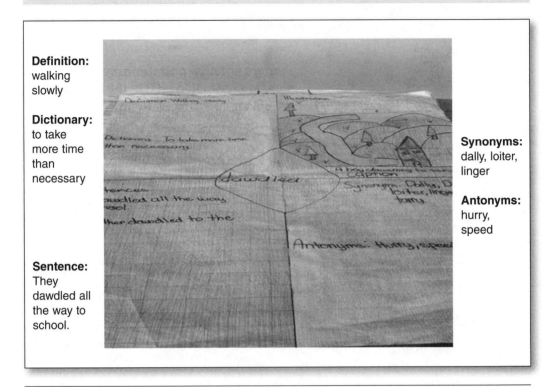

Definition:
walking
slowly

Dictionary:
to take
more time
than
necessary

Synonyms:
dally, loiter,
linger

Antonyms:
hurry,
speed

Sentence:
They
dawdled all
the way to
school.

Source: Soto, 2012.

Notice in this student sample that the target word *dawdled* is defined as: *To take more time than necessary; walking slowly*. Additionally, the visual picture shows a student dawdling to school with the same caption below the photo. Also observe that with this strategy, ELLs can associate many more words (dally, loiter, linger, slowly, more time than necessary) with the target word by completing the exercise, which in turn further expands their vocabulary repertoire. The visual and joint construction of the definition assists students with retention of the target word due to the explicit scaffolding illustrated.

Incorporating Think-Pair-Share Into the Lesson Plan Design

The linkage between academic oral language development and writing was established early in this book. The Think-Pair-Share strategy is a specific oral language and listening scaffold that explicitly demonstrates for students how to speak in the academic register; how to actively listen so that thoughts can be paraphrased; and how to go deeper around meaning once the conversation with a partner produced consensus.

Figure 2.11 Think-Pair-Share Graphic Organizer

Question (Open-ended)	What I Think (Speaking)	What My Partner Thought (Listening)	What We Thought (Consensus)

Source: Education Oasis, 2006.

A Think-Pair-Share graphic organizer template is demonstrated in Figure 2.11 and explained in the paragraph that follows.

The key to incorporating this strategy into teaching practice is to craft open-ended questions that allow students to think critically about the topic and content at hand. Talking about the topic with a partner in this way allows students to create a mental outline for the writing assignment at hand. In essence, this is a way to have students anticipate the topic at hand, and/or allow students to further process the building background knowledge portion of the lesson. Either way, students are building deeper meaning around the topic, which is what they require to write about a topic thoroughly.

Putting It All Together Across Genres of Writing

As noted in Figure 2.12, this section of the book unpacks the three genres of writing addressed in the CCSS. Each genre includes a lesson plan template that scaffolds writing by incorporating academic language development strategies, and moves students from speaking to writing. Each lesson also addresses the text type within a particular content area, including English Language Arts, Science, and History. A series of mentor texts is recommended for each genre of writing, as well as a graphic organizer for unpacking the genre of writing with students. The first lesson begins with the genre of personal narrative, with an emphasis on well-chosen details and well-structured event sequences, all emphasized in the CCSS. The second lesson unpacks the genre of argumentative writing, with an emphasis on supplying sufficient evidence from a variety of sources. The final lesson focuses on informative/explanatory writing in Science, with an emphasis on analyzing data and content. The three CCSS Anchor Standards that are addressed for writing are found in Figure 2.12.

Figure 2.12 Three CCSS Anchor Standards

Writing
1. Write **narratives** to develop real or imagined experiences or events using effective technique, **well-chosen details**, and *well-structured event sequences*.
2. Write **arguments** to support claims in an analysis of substantive topics or texts, using valid reasoning and relevant and *sufficient evidence*.
3. Write **informative/explanatory texts** to examine and convey complex ideas and information clearly and accurately through the *effective selection, organization, and analysis of content*.

Source: NGA & CCSSO, 2010.

3

From Spoken Language to Narrative Writing (Language Arts— Elementary)

PURPOSE

The basic purpose of narrative is to entertain, to gain, and to hold a readers' interest. However, narratives can also be written to teach or inform, to change attitudes and social opinions that are used to raise topical issues. Narratives sequence people and characters in time and place, but unlike recounts, it is through the sequencing that the stories set up one or more problems that must eventually find a way to be resolved. The expectation for narrative writing within the CCSS is that students, "Write narratives to develop real or imagined experiences or events using effective technique, well-chosen details, and well-structured event sequences" (CCSS, 2013). Notice the emphasis here on *well-chosen details* and *well-structured event sequences;* this is a shift from prior narrative writing expectations for students where technique or personal connections were more readily emphasized. The narrative checklist in Figure 3.1 from English Online (2013) is recommended for teachers to teach the elements of narrative writing, preferably dealing a little at a time with mentor texts selections that exemplify each element of the narrative structure.

Figure 3.1 Narrative Structure Checklist

Orientation (first paragraph)
• Where did the story take place?
• When did the story take place?
• How did the story begin?
• Who is in the story?
Complication or Problem
• A description/explanation of the problem.
• The problem usually involves the main character(s).
Resolution
• How the problem has been solved.
Conclusion
• A final concluding statement.
Characterization
• A description of the main characters.
• What do they look like?
Theme
• A clear message.

LANGUAGE

Use Active Verbs
• Instead of "The old woman was in his way"
try
• "The old woman barred his path."
• The first person (I, we)
or
• The third person (he, she, they).
• The past tense is used.
Conjunctions
• Linking words to do with time are used.
Specific Nouns
• oak instead of tree
Use Adjectives and Adverbs
Use the Senses
• What does it smell like?
• What can be heard?

- What can be seen?
- What does it taste like?
- What does it feel like?

- A variety of sentence beginnings are used.

- It has an impact on the reader.
- The personal voice of the writer comes through.

Narratives often use:

Similes

- The sea looked as rumpled as a blue quilted dressing gown.
- The wind wrapped me up like a cloak.

Metaphors

- She has a heart of stone.
- He is a stubborn mule.
- The man barked out the instructions.

Onomatopoeia

- crackle, splat, ooze, squish, boom
- The tires whirr on the road.
- The pitter-patter of soft rain.
- The mud oozed and squished through my toes.

Personification

- The steel beam clenched its muscles.
- Clouds limped across the sky.
- The pebbles on the path were gray with grief.

Source: English Online, 2013.

For the narrative writing task in this section, students write detailed personal narratives about themselves, including well-structured event sequences in order to reflect the ability to transfer those skills to a complex and text-based narrative where evidence from characteristics of characters of a story are included. Since this writing task is scheduled at the beginning of the school year, it also serves as a "get to know you" activity.

The Reading and Writing Connection

In a presentation to the Delaware Department of Education, David Coleman (2012) suggests, "Good writing comes from good reading." As such, each genre of writing begins with an overview of the text type, including the purpose and organization of the text, followed by reading several mentor texts from that genre. By using mentor texts, ELLs have several writing models to review to glean examples for their own writing. In essence, this step assists with building background knowledge of the text type itself so that students are more likely to use and internalize the genre of writing. Some sample mentor texts for personal narratives are included below.

Mentor Texts to Teach Children About Personal Narratives

Salt Hands by Jane Chelsea Aragon

Those Shoes by Maribeth Boelts

Fireflies by Judy Brinckloe

Bigmama's by Donald Crews

Shortcut by Donald Crews

When I Was Your Age by Amy Erlich

Roller Coaster by Marla Frazee

The Leaving Morning by Angela Johnson

The Snowy Day by Ezra Jack Keats

Saturday and Teacakes by Lester Laminach

What You Know First by Patricia Maclachlin

Coat of Many Colors by Dolly Parton

The Paperboy by Dav Pilkey

Chicken Sunday by Patricia Polacco

Mrs. Mack by Patricia Polacco

The Relatives Came by Cynthia Rylant

When I Was Young in the Mountains by Cynthia Rylant

Night Shift Daddy by Eileen Spinelli

Knuffle Bunny by Mo Willems

The Other Side by Jacqueline Woodson

Every Friday by Dan Yaccarino

Building Background Knowledge of the Text Type

After teachers read several mentor texts with the class, students complete the graphic organizer in Figure 3.2, which requires them to think through the characteristics of the narrative genre. Then students must substantiate the evidence for the narrative genre by identifying specific quotes from the text that support that text type. The teacher models how to use the graphic organizer by completing each section with the class after reading their first text together.

Figure 3.2 Blank Text Type Graphic Organizer

Name of Text: _____

Characteristics of narrative genre in this text: _____

_____

_____

_____

I know this is a narrative text because (use specific quotes as evidence . . .)

_____

_____

_____

Source: Soto, 2012.

ELLs also benefit when time is dedicated to talk about each of the sections of the graphic organizer. In essence, the last statement becomes an academic language stem for the genre of writing and can extend the discourse by using evidence from the text. For the purposes of this personal narrative writing lesson, students select and read together as a class one of the texts listed in bold from the above list of model mentor texts. The sample graphic organizer in Figure 3.3 was completed using the text, *When I Was Young in the Mountains* by Cynthia Rylant (1982). One proposal is that students keep a writing portfolio of mentor text types so that they can utilize them as resources and have them available when they begin to write. By writing down evidence of different characteristics of the writing text type, students also begin to use these techniques as they craft their own writing.

This text was selected as the first mentor text for this genre, because the repetition of the phrase, "When I was young in the mountains . . . " helps ELLs to unpack the sequence of events in the personal narrative.

PERSONAL NARRATIVE LESSON PLAN

Figure 3.4 is a design for the personal narrative writing genre lesson plan incorporating the academic language development strategies introduced in the first chapter of the book. This lesson is designed for the third grade with an emphasis on personal narratives.

Figure 3.3 Example Text Type Graphic Organizer

Name of Text: *When I Was Young in the Mountains* by Cynthia Rylant

Characteristics of Narrative Genre in this text:

Sequence people/characters in time and place; consistent use of the phrase, "When I was young in the mountains" to denote time and place; tells who, where, and when; includes a series of events; use of first person for personal narrative.

I know this is a narrative text because (use specific quotes as evidence . . .)

Use of "When I was young in the mountains . . . " to describe sequence of events. Examples include, "When I was young in the mountains, Grandmother spread the table with hot corn bread, pinto beans, and fried okra" and "When I was young in the mountains, we pumped pails of water from the well at the bottom of the hill, and heated the water to fill round tin tubs for our baths."

Figure 3.4 Personal Narrative Lesson Plan

Grade:	3rd Grade
Writing Genre/Objective	• **Personal Narratives***:* Write narratives to develop real or imagined experiences or events using effective technique, well-chosen details, and well-structured event sequences. • **Meme**: Students create a meme about themselves (Who my friends think I am; Who my mom thinks I am; Who my teachers think I am; Who society thinks I am; Who I think I am; Who I really am), which they use to write a narrative to teach others about themselves.
Purpose	• **To Entertain, to Teach**

Organization	• **Orientation (tells who, where, when)**
	  o Series of Events
	  o Problem
	  o Resolution

Connectives	• **To Do With Time** (first, then, next, afterwards, at the end of the day)

Other Linguistic Features	• **Past Tense**
	  o Tells about what happened
	  o Action Verbs
	  o May have dialogue and verbs of "saying"

Building Background Knowledge for Content of Writing	• **Use of Mentor Text:** *When I Was Young in the Mountains* to teach about the elements of a personal narrative.

Grade:	3rd Grade
	• **Use of Teacher's Meme:** and personal narrative as a model text type.
Academic Oral Language Development (Think-Pair-Share With Open-ended Questions)	• Who do you think society thinks you are? • Who do you think you are? • Who are you really? • Interview your friends, family, and teacher about who they think you are.
Specialized Vocabulary Needed (Frayer Model)	Narrative writing, meme, sequence of events, perceptions

It is always best to encourage students to begin with a writing genre and topic that is familiar to them. Oftentimes, ELLs are familiar with the narrative structure because of a culture replete with oral traditions (e.g., ELLs from Spanish speaking countries are told *cuentos* or *leyendas*), consequently this background knowledge can be tapped into around this writing genre. Starting with this genre of writing at the beginning of the school year is also a great "get to know you" and building community activity. In addition, because students are creating their own memes, this activity connects them to culturally relevant topics (the Internet and online content) that replicate their interests and background knowledge. Finally, by connecting to technology, teachers are also working on their 21st century skills.

The teacher begins the lesson by asking the students to develop their own meme; this is then extended into a personal narrative writing assignment emphasizing detail and sequence of events. The purpose of both the meme and the personal narrative is that through these vehicles, both the class and the teacher learn about the student. To initiate this lesson, the teacher asks open-ended questions with the Think-Pair-Share strategy, introduces the vocabulary word *meme* and the phrase *sequence of events*, and uses these target words to connect directly to the first part of the lesson. The teacher then shows a series of memes that she downloaded from the Internet, especially ones that depict a person's personality or traits (A website used to find and generate memes is http://memegenerator .net/). Once students create their memes, they both write about them and present them to the class, as part of a larger "get to know you" assignment at the beginning of the school year. Memes are also a useful tool to create for characters in a story, which is described later in this section.

Frayer Model: Building Background Knowledge Around Memes

Once a series of memes are shown to the class, the teacher asks students to discuss what the memes have in common, and how they depict

Figure 3.5 Frayer Model: Definition of Meme

DEFINITION	VISUAL/PICTURE
A meme is a culturally familiar picture with a concept or message about someone or something that is spread on the Internet, in order to publicize particular ideas.	

Target Word: Meme

EXAMPLES/MODELS	NON-EXAMPLES
• Picture with a key text that says something funny about someone. • Concept or idea about someone or something that is spread on Internet. • A way to publicize ideas on the Internet.	• An advertisement not on the Internet or widely displayed. • A regular photo without text. • A visual that does not tell a specific story.

particular messages about the characters or pictures displayed. Once students discuss this question in partners, they can share out responses with the whole class, and fill out the Frayer model graphic organizer together. Some examples of students sharing the meaning of their memes are depicted in Figure 3.8.

Both the examples and non-examples sections are elicited from a classroom and/or partner conversation about the pictures that the teacher shows. Students then develop their own picture, which in this case is one of the memes that the teacher showed the class. The picture presents a visual scaffold for students to recall the word. Finally, as a class, the teacher and students use examples in order to write a classroom definition of the word. Students can also choose to write their own definition, after the class definition has been developed.

Figure 3.6 is another example of the Frayer model with the second target phrase for this writing assignment, which is *sequence of events*. Sequence of events is a key element of the narrative genre, and as such it is important for students to begin practicing this feature early in the school year.

Since students create their own meme displaying elements of themselves in a particular order (i.e., how society, and their friends and parents view them), it is doubly important that this target vocabulary phrase is fully comprehended and mastered.

After the class defines the phrase *sequence of events*, it is important to have a conversation about how this applies to the meme that students develop. It should be emphasized that the sequence of events is important to the order of the story; the meme has a particular sequence: for example, who my friends, parents, boss, society, and I think I am. The sequence begins with who others think I am and then ends with who I think I am.

Academic Oral Language Development: Think-Pair-Share

Once the target words are defined with the whole class, students can then utilize the Think-Pair-Share organizer to thoughtfully respond to the questions regarding the sequence of events about themselves. Notice that by thinking through these questions individually first—these are huge life questions after all—students can then respond deeply and thoughtfully with a partner. If students did not have time to think, speak, and listen first, they might just write the first thing on their minds instead of the most accurate and self-reflective response. The Think-Pair-Share strategy holds students accountable for introspection and critical thinking. The process also requires students to speak and listen carefully, thereby working on all four literacy domains.

Figure 3.6   Frayer Model: Definition of Phrase–Sequence of Events

DEFINITION	VISUAL/PICTURE
The sequence of events includes details and specifics about the order of events in a story.	1, 2, 3, 4 . . . First, second, third, last . . .
EXAMPLES/MODELS	**NON-EXAMPLES**
• The sequential or numerical order that an event occurs. • Details and specifics about the order of events. • Textual evidence/support for the order of events.	• Random order. • No order. • Little details of events.

Target Phrase: Sequence of Events

Figure 3.7 Think-Pair-Share Graphic Organizer

Question (Open-ended)	What I Think (Speaking)	What My Partner Thought (Listening)	What We Thought (Consensus)
1. Who do you think society thinks you are?			
2. Who do you think you are?			
3. Who are you really?			

Source: Education Oasis, 2006.

Once students share their thoughts with a partner concerning the above three questions, they can interview their parents and friends about who they (parents and friends) think they are. After these questions are answered, the teacher then shares her own meme, orally describing what each of the pictures tells about her. For example, "*My meme demonstrates there are many facets to who I am, and what different people in my life think that I do. For example, the first picture shows that many of my friends think that teachers spend a lot of their time reading to students. Although this may be true, other people, like my Mom, put my profession up on a pedestal and may think that I spend all of my time mentoring and investing in students. My boss, on the other hand, may think that I spend most of my time presenting to groups of people at conferences, while society thinks that I spend my time writing books. What I really spend a lot of time doing, however, is trying to live a balanced life by doing the things that I love most like hiking, spending time with family and friends, and enjoying good food and drinks.*"

After developing their own memes, practicing presentations in small groups and partners, and presenting the memes to the whole class, students use their meme as a scaffold for writing their own personal narratives. Namely, students write what they described orally, in the order of the meme sequence, to develop a personal narrative. Students are then able to create a meme and write a personal narrative about a character from a story. For example, after having read *When I Was Young in the Mountains,* students can develop a meme around the portrayal of the main character by inferring how society, her boss, and her parents view her. Students need to provide specific support for their ideas from the text, and then can write a personal narrative about the character, again using the meme sequence of events to scaffold the writing process.

Figure 3.8 Personal Meme

Source: Adapted from http://memegenerator.net/

From Spoken Language to Argumentative Writing (History— High School)

Whether narrative or argumentative, a common thread throughout the CCSS genres of writing is making evidence-based claims. For the argumentative genre of writing, it is important for students to know their own argument inside out, as well as to thoroughly know the counterarguments so that they effectively support their position. The reason to understand counterarguments to a claim is that it demonstrates that a student knows the topic well enough to refute the other side of a claim. Correspondingly, knowing both sides of a claim also assists students with understanding multiple perspectives and various points of view, which then transfers when students are expected to collaborate and "work respectfully with diverse teams" (CCSS, 2013). In essence, students learn how to have an academic disagreement or cognitive dissonance as well as how to respond objectively.

RELIABLE VERSUS UNRELIABLE SOURCES

One of the key instructional shifts with the CCSS is "Focus on reading, writing, and speaking that is grounded in evidence collected from multiple sources" (CCSS, 2013). In the genre of argumentation, students must support their claims with ample and reliable evidence, which means that they must find a variety of reliable sources to support their claims. In this way, the expectations within the CCSS is that students integrate a variety of sources, including multiple texts and resources, which in turn teach them to present well-defended claims, clear information, and analyses to their argument.

In order to achieve this expectation, determining what is and is not a reliable source must also be taught explicitly. The teacher presents a mini lesson that involves students analyzing reliable versus unreliable sources. An assortment of online sources for a topic can be preselected, and a discussion regarding the elements of reliable sources can follow. This assists students with the metacognition about which sources are reliable and which are not, while also giving them concrete examples of those sources for future reference. A T-chart like the one shown in Figure 4.1 can assist students with determining the reliability and unreliability of their selected sources.

GENRE APPROACH TO ARGUMENTATIVE WRITING

The following chart describes the essential characteristics of argumentation to address as students learn this text type. As was the case when discussing the narrative genre, it is imperative to review with the students each characteristic of the text type, including purpose, organization, and the linguistic features. Additionally, present the students with model texts. As an example, the argumentative letter found in Figure 4.2 was written by a teacher as a text type model, and is used for the lesson in this section. The letter was written by a fictional colleague of Albert Einstein, a Mr. Heinrich Hauser from the University of Berlin, who is trying to persuade the famous scientist to return to Germany during the time period of the rise of the Nazi party.

Figure 4.1 T-Chart Reliable Versus Unreliable Structure

Reliable Sources (with justification)	Unreliable Sources (with justification)
• Peer-reviewed article because it has gone through review from experts in the field. • Webpage developed by researchers or experts from a particular field because they have evidence to substantiate claims.	• Wikipedia, unless you go back to the original source, which must also be analyzed. • Personal blog because it is subjective opinion.

Figure 4.2 Model Argumentative Letter

University of Berlin
founded 1624

My Dear Albert,

We have just been informed by the physics department chair that you have decided to stay in the United States, and not return to the University of Berlin.

I am appalled that you would desert your homeland at this time! Your colleagues and I have discussed your decision and want you to reconsider your obvious error in judgment.

First of all, what possible function could you fulfill at Princeton University? You must know Americans are only journeymen scientists and will use this opportunity to exploit your intellect to foster their own goals.

Secondly, what kind of collegial stimulation can you encounter there? All of your fellow scientists and friends are here in Germany. Are there any noted scientists in the United States? Apparently, the Wright Brothers are the best that they can produce.

Lastly, the United States is devoid of culture. How can you compare Mark Twain to Goethe? You will be intellectually suffocated in that sterile, puritanical environment.

Albert, think again! We are on the brink of amazing and world shaking discoveries in Germany. You need to be a part of this. Do not be seduced by promises of money and celebrity. It is an obvious ploy to convince you to stay in the United States.

Your Colleague,
Heinrich Hauser, PhD
Department of Physics, University of Berlin

Source: Line, 2002.

The teacher reads the model argumentative letter and reviews and compares with the students the elements of argumentation from Figure 4.3. After the letter is read, students underline the elements of the argumentation in pairs (as demonstrated below) so that they can begin to identify those elements of argumentation when reading, as well as incorporate them into their own writing.

After students identify and underline the elements of argumentation in the model argumentative letter (see Figure 4.4), they then write a response to the letter, writing as Albert Einstein, using evidence they analyzed from primary source documents (note: this element is further explained later in this chapter). It is also important to acknowledge that argumentative

Figure 4.3 Elements of Argumentation

Discussion (one side)
Argument (two sides)
(e.g., Should smoking be made illegal?)
Purpose To persuade others to take a position and justify it.
Organization • Personal statement of position • Argument(s) and supporting evidence • Possibly counterargument(s) and supporting evidence • Conclusion
Connectives • First • Second • In addition • Therefore • However • On the other hand
Other Linguistic Features May use argumentative language (e.g., It is obviously wrong, it is clearly stupid that . . .)

Source: Gibbons, 2002.

writing regains importance within the CCSS, so it is essential for students to become skilled at this genre of writing. The letter in Figure 4.4 includes annotations by the students to highlight the elements of argumentation they detected.

MOVING FROM ARGUMENTATIVE SPEAKING TO WRITING

According to the ELP Framework,

> Students must read, write, view, and visually represent as they develop their models and explanations. They *speak and listen* as they present their ideas or engage in *reasoned argumentation* with others to *refine their ideas and reach shared conclusions.* As students *analyze examples of arguments,* they learn the characteristics of a *strong scientific justification of a claim* and they learn to *identify weak*

support. As they argue with others to arrive at a shared 'best' explanation or model, they are motivated to *clarify both their language and their thinking* by the atmosphere of shared interest and goals. (Council of Chief State School Officers, 2012, p. 4)

This quote is a reminder of the important skills and concepts (which have been italicized) that ELLs must learn in order to become experts at argumentative writing. Notice that the notion of moving from speaking to writing—that is through academic oral argumentation first—requires that ELLs continue to refine and clarify their thinking in order to achieve the best spoken and written efforts.

Figure 4.4   Model of Argumentative Letter With Annotations

University of Berlin
founded 1624

My Dear Albert,

We have just been informed by the physics department chair that you have decided to stay in the United States, and not return to the University of Berlin.

<u>I am appalled that you would desert your homeland at this time!</u> Your colleagues and I have discussed your decision and want you to reconsider your <u>obvious error in judgment</u>.

<u>First of all</u>, what possible function could you fulfill at Princeton University? You must know Americans are only <u>journeymen scientists</u> and will use this opportunity to <u>exploit your intellect</u> to foster their own goals.

<u>Secondly</u>, what kind of collegial stimulation can you encounter there? All of your fellow scientists and friends are here in Germany. <u>Are there any noted scientists in the United States?</u> Apparently, the Wright Brothers are the best that they can produce.

<u>Lastly</u>, the United States is devoid of culture. <u>How can you compare Mark Twain to Goethe?</u> You will be intellectually suffocated in that sterile, puritanical environment.

Albert, think again! <u>We are on the brink of amazing and world shaking discoveries in Germany.</u> You need to be a part of this. Do not be seduced by promises of money and celebrity. It is an obvious ploy to convince you to stay in the United States.

Your Colleague,

Heinrich Hauser, PhD

Department of Physics, University of Berlin

Source: Line, 2002.

In this section, the cycle of clarifying language and thinking using Think-Pair-Share and the Frayer model are used with the model lesson on argumentative writing. Group work is also recommended as students analyze primary source documents from the rise of the Nazi Party in Germany. Students develop academic language related to historical interpretation

Figure 4.5   Curriculum Cycle Lesson Plan for Argumentative Writing in History

Grade:	10th Grade
Common Core State Standard	Write arguments to support claims in an analysis of substantive topics or texts, using valid reasoning and relevant and sufficient evidence.
Writing Objective	Students develop academic language related to historical interpretation and write an argumentative letter.
Objective	Students begin to build background knowledge about the impact of German anti-Jewish propaganda by analyzing primary source documents from the time period.
Purpose	To persuade others, to take a position and justify it.
Organization	• Personal statement of position • Argument(s) and supporting evidence • Possibly counterargument(s) and supporting evidence • Conclusion
Connectives	First, second, in addition, therefore, however, on the other hand
Other Linguistic Features	May use argumentative language (e.g., it is obviously wrong, it is clearly an issue that . . .)
Building Background Knowledge for Content of Writing	• Primary source document analysis from rise of World War II • Sample argumentative letter • Instructional read aloud about Albert Einstein
Academic Oral Language development (Think-Pair-Share With Open-ended Questions)	• What would make a person leave their country and never want to return? • How did Einstein not fit into the educational setting of his time?
Specialized Vocabulary Needed (Frayer Model)	Persuasion, propaganda, alien, abolition, self-determination.

Source: Soto, 2012.

and write an argumentative response to Heinrich Hauser's letter found in the previous sections. Students build background knowledge about the impact of German anti-Jewish propaganda by analyzing primary source documents from that time period. Students also learn about the life of Albert Einstein, a German Jew, in order to connect to a historical figure from this time period. Students are asked to then put all of these pieces together by writing an argumentative letter incorporating primary source evidence, as if they were Albert Einstein writing back to Heinrich Hauser, his colleague at the University of Berlin. The lesson plan below details each of the elements of this lesson that are scaffolded for language and content.

Think-Pair-Share in Argumentative Writing

The lesson begins by having students Think-Pair-Share about the first open-ended question presented: What would make a person leave their country and never want to return? It is important for students to respond to the question and to consider the notion of never wanting to return to one's home country, which of course is an extreme situation. A sample academic conversation about this question is included in Figure 4.6. Students are reminded to begin their responses with academic language stems (included in the Appendix).

As students are involved in their Think-Pair-Share discussions, the teacher power walks around the room and listens for accountable conversations as well as appropriate responses that can be shared with the entire class. These responses can then be listed on the board as reasons why someone like Albert Einstein might leave his country during the time

Figure 4.6 Think-Pair-Share Organizer With Academic Language Stems

Question (Open-ended)	What I Think (Speaking)	What My Partner Thought (Listening)	What We Thought (Consensus)
What would make a person leave their country and never want to return?	It seems to me that it would be an extreme situation for someone to leave their country and not want to return. Maybe the person feels unsafe?	I hear you saying that it's not a little reason that someone would leave and not return, and that maybe it's because they are unsafe.	We both thought that someone would leave their home country and never return due to an extreme situation.

Source: Soto, 2012.

period of the rise of the Nazi party in Germany. The teacher ties the ideas that emerge to introduce the concepts that are under study throughout the lesson, including genocide, the Holocaust, and issues of religious freedom during this time period.

Frayer Model in Argumentative Writing

In this portion of the lesson, students are introduced to the key words that they need to know (primary source document, argumentation, and Holocaust) in order to analyze the primary source documents. The words introduced here are also incorporated into the argumentative letter that they write, as well as used in spoken language. In essence, students are held accountable for using the words in spoken and written language once they make it to the Frayer model graphic organizer and classroom posters. An example (Figure 4.7) of the Frayer model using one of the unit words, *propaganda,* is completed below, along with the building background segment developed to define the word.

BUILDING BACKGROUND KNOWLEDGE AROUND ACADEMIC VOCABULARY

In order to build background knowledge around the word *propaganda,* students explored the United States Holocaust Memorial Museum website (http://www.ushmm.org/propaganda/). Here, students analyzed examples of propaganda from the time period under study. After 5 to 10 minutes of exploring the Gallery section (upper right hand corner of the website), students are asked about the commonalities in the primary source documents that they reviewed, and as a class, they are asked to define the target word, *propaganda.*

After each of the key words (primary source document, argumentation, and Holocaust) for the unit are defined and discussed using the Frayer model graphic organizer, students are held accountable for using the words in both spoken and written language, including their argumentative response.

Building Background Knowledge Around Einstein: Substantive Texts

Since the students have to write a letter embodying Albert Einstein's voice and character, they first build some background knowledge around the time period of this lesson for vocabulary development, they then continue by building background knowledge around Einstein's life. For the purpose of this lesson, I recommend that teachers show a video from a PBS

Figure 4.7 Frayer Model: Target Word of Propaganda

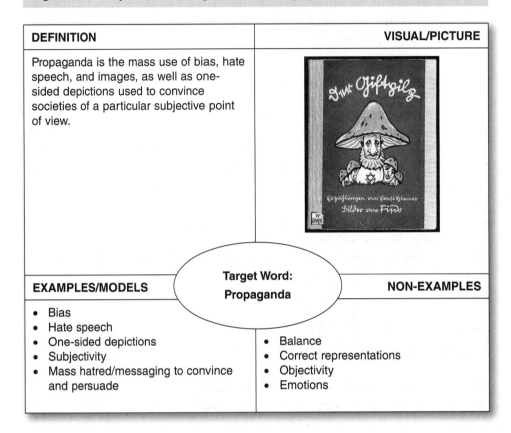

DEFINITION	VISUAL/PICTURE
Propaganda is the mass use of bias, hate speech, and images, as well as one-sided depictions used to convince societies of a particular subjective point of view.	

Target Word: Propaganda

EXAMPLES/MODELS	NON-EXAMPLES
• Bias • Hate speech • One-sided depictions • Subjectivity • Mass hatred/messaging to convince and persuade	• Balance • Correct representations • Objectivity • Emotions

series called "Einstein Revealed" (http://www.pbs.org/wgbh/nova/physics/einstein-revealed.html). Teachers may also choose to use an excerpt from Joy Hakim's American History textbook series called *A History of US: Finding the Stories in Science and History* (Hakim, 2003). Hakim writes science and history textbooks from the perspective of historical figures, which allows the reader to engage in the content much more readily due to the characterizations. The chapter called "A Boy With Something on His Mind" is about Albert Einstein as a child and young adult, before his scientific discoveries. The chapter presents the struggles that Einstein faced in school and allows a high school student to identify with how he did not fit into the educational system. Students might also identify with the fact that Einstein learned best by discussing ideas and through hands-on experiences, not by lecture or rote memorization. As the teacher reads aloud segments of the text, students should actively listen for and write down specific ways that Einstein did not fit into the educational system. During this process, students should use the graphic organizer shown in Figure 4.8, where they also can collect and record additional information for this lesson.

Figure 4.8 Response Journal

First Response (quick write)	How did Einstein not fit into the educational system? A.
Second Response (word wall connection)	B. C.
Third Response (What question would you like to ask the artist?)	D.

As the teacher delivers the instructional read aloud on the life of Einstein as a student, she can stop throughout and have students share reasons why Einstein did not fit into his educational system. At the end of the read aloud, the class can brainstorm key ways to incorporate Einstein's voice and this background information into the argumentative letter response, using evidence from the text.

ANALYZING PRIMARY SOURCE DOCUMENTS

At this point, students are now ready to analyze primary source documents in groups. Groups of four should be carefully selected with assurance that ELLs have linguistic models in their groups. These heterogeneous groups can include two mid-range students, one high, and one low. This allows for a variety of conversations and interactions between students so that the ELL in a group has linguistic models to emulate, while higher end students also have someone to interact with at the midrange level.

Once groups are established, students return to the United States Holocaust Memorial Museum website that they reviewed for building background knowledge. This time, the teacher models analyzing a primary source document from the website with the class using the document analysis graphic organizer adapted from the Library of Congress.

The focus of the document analysis organizer is to assist students with thinking and reviewing documents as a historian. This review also allows

Figure 4.9   Document Analysis Sheet

Document Letter or Number: _____ Source: _____ Author: _____

Date: _____ Primary Source: _____ Secondary Source: _____

Key Quote, Image, or Data: _____

_____

_____

Main Idea of Document: _____

_____

Source: Adapted from Library of Congress, 2013.

students to make objective and evidence-based conclusions about documents from this time period. Specifically, when analyzing primary sources, students answer two key questions:

1. What is the key quote, image, or data provided by the document?

2. What is the main idea of this key quote, image, or data?

First, the teacher models analyzing the primary source document together as a class, using the think aloud technique. She also demonstrates for students how to use the graphic organizer to answer the two focus questions. For example, the teacher might say, "*I can see that the translation for the text on the primary source document tells me that this is a cover of an anti-Semitic schoolbook titled 'The Poisonous Mushroom.' Since that is the key quote, I take that down in the first section of my graphic organizer. As evidence of that, I write down that the major image is the mushroom with the Star of David in the middle of its body.*"

To answer the second question regarding the main idea of a quote or image, the teacher might use a think aloud to respond, "*It seems to me that since the title is 'The Poisonous Mushroom,' that Jews are being depicted as poisonous to society. Since the mushroom has a Star of David on its chest, Jews are being depicted as a fungus or inhuman.*" By modeling how to use the document analysis form, students are provided with a way to make objective statements about the primary source documents that they review in groups.

Figure 4.10   The Poisonous Mushroom

Source: United States Holocaust Memorial Museum, 2012. Used with permission.

Productive Group Work

Once students have a model for analyzing a primary source document, they analyze three more primary source documents in groups on their own. The teacher should put students in heterogeneous groups of three or four, with ELLs included in groups so that they have a language model. Students then select three additional primary source documents from the Holocaust Museum website that they want to analyze together in a group using the document analysis sheet. The group must come to consensus about their analysis and each student should also complete their own document analysis sheet. It is important to remind students that these primary source documents are evidence in their argumentative response to Heinrich Hauser, telling why it is unsafe for Albert Einstein to return to Germany. The student discussions about the three primary source documents that they reviewed in groups, should answer the two key questions: 1) what is the key quote, image, or data provided by the document? 2) what is the main idea of this key quote, image, or data?

Putting It All Together

Once students accumulate all of the pieces necessary to write their argumentative letter, including building background knowledge about key vocabulary and Albert Einstein as well as analyzing primary source documents as evidence, they are ready to begin writing their response to Heinrich Hauser's argumentative letter. At this point, the elements of argumentative writing should be reviewed once again, using both the model letter and the argumentative writing chart.

Since the teacher has modeled analyzing the primary source document, "The Poisonous Mushroom," she can model for students how she

Figure 4.11   Model Argumentative Letter

University of Berlin
founded 1624

My Dear Albert,

We have just been informed by the physics department chair that you have decided to stay in the United States, and not return to the University of Berlin.

I am appalled that you would desert your homeland at this time! Your colleagues and I have discussed your decision and want you to reconsider your obvious error in judgment.

First of all, what possible function could you fulfill at Princeton University? You must know Americans are only journeymen scientists and will use this opportunity to exploit your intellect to foster their own goals.

Secondly, what kind of collegial stimulation can you encounter there? All of your fellow scientists and friends are here in Germany. Are there any noted scientists in the United States? Apparently, the Wright Brothers are the best that they can produce.

Lastly, the United States is devoid of culture. How can you compare Mark Twain to Goethe? You will be intellectually suffocated in that sterile, puritanical environment.

Albert, think again! We are on the brink of amazing and world shaking discoveries in Germany. You need to be a part of this. Do not be seduced by promises of money and celebrity. It is an obvious ploy to convince you to stay in the United States.

Your Colleague,
Heinrich Hauser, PhD
Department of Physics, University of Berlin

Source: Line, 2002.

Figure 4.12 Model Rebuttal Letter

My Dearest Heinrich,

I recently received your letter and I appreciate your concern. Appalled? Homeland? I cannot consider Germany my homeland when I am looked at as a poisonous mushroom! I am not a fungus that will bring the demise of Germany, but a productive member of society, who can make many scientific contributions! In the United States and at Princeton, I am free to pursue and contribute in ways that would be impossible in Germany right now. Heinrich, you think again! Think about what you are asking me to sacrifice—my very life.

might begin the first portion of her response to Heinrich Hauser as Albert Einstein, using a think aloud to include that specific children's book cover. It might start as shown in Figure 4.12 (above).

This model introductory paragraph serves as a jumping-off place for writing with students. A further differentiation for ELLs could be that they write collaboratively in a group, with each student taking on a particular element of the writing. For example, one student could be responsible for incorporating the elements of argumentation from the chart, while another student is responsible for incorporating each of the primary source documents. Finally, a third student could be in charge of making certain that each of Heinrich Hauser's points are addressed from the original letter. Collaborative writing is a good way to apprentice students to the expectations of writing within a particular genre, especially if it is their first exposure. It is important, however, to gradually release the writing to each student so that eventually they complete their own writing piece.

5 From Spoken Language to Informational Writing (Science— Middle School)

The National Research Council (NRC) set forth a vision for what it means to be proficient in Science by laying out a framework to guide teachers called the Next Generation Science Standards (NGSS) (Achieve, 2013). Similar to the integration of language and content within the CCSS, the three dimensions of the NGSS encompass the following elements:

- Dimension 1: Practices—these practices describe the behaviors that scientists engage in during scientific inquiry.
- Dimension 2: Crosscutting Concepts—are the concepts that have connections or overlap across all domains of science.
- Dimension 3: Disciplinary Core Ideas—these core ideas focus on the most important aspects of science across the K–12 science curriculum (Achieve, 2013).

For the informational writing lesson in this chapter, students will begin the process of designing a garden at their school site. The lesson that follows is the first of a series of lessons that will eventually address

Figure 5.1 NGSS Chart

Practices	Disciplinary Core Ideas	Crosscutting Concepts
Asking Questions and Defining Problems Asking questions and defining problems in Grades 6–8 builds on Grades K–5 experiences and progresses to specifying relationships between variables, and clarifying arguments and models. Ask questions to identify and clarify evidence of an argument. (MS-ESS3–5) **Constructing Explanations and Designing Solutions** Constructing explanations and designing solutions in Grades 6–8 builds on the experiences in K–5 and progresses to include constructing explanations and designing solutions supported by multiple sources of evidence consistent with scientific ideas, principles, and theories. Construct a scientific explanation based on valid and reliable evidence obtained from sources (including the students' own experiments) and the assumption that theories and laws that describe the natural world operate today as they did in the past and will continue to do so in the future. (MS-ESS3–1) Apply scientific principles to design an object, tool, process, or system. (MS-ESS3–3) **Engaging in Argument From Evidence** Engaging in argument from evidence in Grades 6–8 builds on Grades K–5 experiences and progresses to constructing a convincing argument that supports or refutes claims for either explanations or solutions about the natural and designed world(s). Construct an oral and written argument supported by empirical evidence and scientific reasoning to support or refute an explanation or a model for a phenomenon or a solution to a problem. (MS-ESS3–4)	**ESS3.A: Natural Resources** Humans depend on Earth's land, ocean, atmosphere, and biosphere for many different resources. Minerals, fresh water, and biosphere resources are limited, and many are not renewable or replaceable over human lifetimes. These resources are distributed unevenly around the planet as a result of past geologic processes. (MS-ESS3–1) **ESS3.C: Human Impacts on Earth Systems** Human activities have significantly altered the biosphere, sometimes damaging or destroying natural habitats and causing the extinction of other species. But changes to Earth's environments can have different impacts (negative and positive) for different living things. (MS-ESS3–3) Typically as human populations and per capita consumption of natural resources increase, so do the negative impacts on Earth unless the activities and technologies involved are engineered otherwise. (MS-ESS3–3), (MS-ESS3–4)	**Patterns** Graphs, charts, and images can be used to identify patterns in data. (MS-ESS3–2)

Source: Achieve, 2013.

the NGSS outlined in the chart below, as students will build an urban garden throughout the school year at their own school site. Notice especially how the practices outlined in the chart align with the CCSS practices for English Language Arts (ELA) addressed thus far. The numbers listed in parentheses refer to specific standards for the study of science found in the Next Generation Study of Science Standards (Achieve, 2013).

These standards are addressed in depth as we progress through the garden unit. To begin, students assemble background knowledge around designing and building a school garden. Specifically, they learn about natural resources and human consumption, as well as sustainability and how gardens connect to our daily nutritional decisions. Students ask questions about their environment, design a local solution to issues in their environment, and construct a written argument for that solution by incorporating multiple sources.

INFORMATIONAL WRITING EXPECTATIONS

The lesson plan organizer in Figure 5.2 outlines the specific content connected to informational writing. The end goal of this lesson is for students to write an informational essay using the multiple sources they reviewed describing the kind of garden they want to have at their school. It is important to note that the informational writing genre accounts for 4 percent of the writing expectations within the CCSS, so ample exposure to writing this text type is important (Achieve, 2013).

Building Linguistic Knowledge

The teacher begins by explaining the characteristics of an informational essay using Figure 5.3 as a guide. Just as in previous chapters, it is important for teachers to explain the purpose, organization, connectives and other linguistic tools associated with this genre of writing. These elements of writing are then posted in the room for reference throughout the unit of study.

Building Content Knowledge

Once the above characteristics for informational writing are reviewed with students, it is time to begin building the field or building background knowledge about the selected subject content. The teacher begins by showing a short video about the New York High Line, which is an above ground railway that has been repurposed into an urban garden space in Manhattan. This brief National Geographic video on the High

Figure 5.2 Lesson Plan Organizer

Grade:	8th Grade
Writing Genre Objective	Informational Writing Write informative/explanatory texts to examine and convey complex ideas and information clearly and accurately through the effective selection, organization, and analysis of content.
Writing Objective	Students develop academic language related to environmental science by writing an informational essay about the importance of, including steps toward, building a school garden.
Objective	Students read and review a variety of informational texts about gardens. Students then write an informational essay about the benefits of and elements that they want to include as they design their own school garden.
Purpose	To explain how to complete something
Organization	Goal Steps in sequence
Connectives	First, second, third, finally, etc.
Other Linguistic Features	Uses verbs to give instructions (e.g., take, mix, add, chop, bake, etc.)
Building Background Knowledge for Content of Writing	Students review a variety of written and online texts to examine the benefits of school gardens.
Academic Oral Language Development (Think-Pair-Share With Open-ended Questions)	After reviewing the White House garden layout, what kind of layout do you want to consider for your school garden? How do you creatively see using your garden space (e.g., High Line in New York City, which is a 1-mile linear park built on a 1.45-mile section of the elevated former New York Central Railroad spur)? What kinds of fruits and/or vegetables would you like to plant? Do they connect to the MyPlate Food Pyramid (illustrates the five food groups that are the building blocks for a healthy diet using a familiar image—a place setting for a meal) and how?
Specialized Vocabulary Needed (Frayer Model)	Garden layout, soil health, master gardeners, food pyramid, to name a few.

Line begins to give students creative ideas about using urban spaces, including their own school grounds as they design and build their school garden (High Line, 2011). After watching the video and introducing a

Figure 5.3 Characteristics of an Informational Essay

Procedure/Informational
(e.g., How to make a healthy meal?)
Purpose: To describe how to complete or execute something
Organization   • Goal   • Steps in sequence
Connectives   • First   • Second   • Third   • Finally, to name a few
Other Linguistic Tools   May use verbs to give instructions (e.g., take, mix, add, chop, bake, etc.)

Source: Gibbons, 2002.

Think-Pair-Share discussion using open-ended questions, students read a brief National Geographic article called, "Miracle Above Manhattan" to learn more about the history and design elements of the urban garden space (Goldberger, 2011).

Once students watch the video and read the article, they complete the Think-Pair-Share organizer. Figure 5.4 records how student conversations might sound.

After their initial Think-Pair-Share conversation about space for gardens, students go online to review the layout for the White House garden (Lee, 2009) and First Lady Michelle Obama's 2013 website, *Let's Move!* This website is an excellent resource for helpful information on the development of the White House garden. Once the class reviews these materials, thus increasing their background knowledge about gardens, they are ready to define the target phrase, *garden layout,* with the teacher facilitating this exercise using the Frayer model process (see the example in Figure 5.5).

Once students define the words, *garden layout,* they then begin the process of discussions with their partners about the kind of layout they want for their own school garden, including the space and sunlight requirements. A partner conversation might go as shown in Figure 5.6.

The last two pieces of research that students review to develop their own garden is the school garden checklist from First Lady Michelle Obama's *Let's Move!* website (Let's Move!, 2013), as well as a section on the

Figure 5.4 Think-Pair-Share Organizer 1: Garden Unit

Question (Open-ended)	What I Think (Speaking)	What My Partner Thought (Listening)	What We Thought (Consensus)
How do you creatively see using our garden space at school (i.e., High Line in New York)?	Watching the video made me realize that gardens can be developed in different spaces, so maybe we don't have to have them in the ground.	I agree with you, Miguel. I never realized we could use an abandoned space for a garden. We should go around the school to see where a garden could go.	We both agreed that a garden space doesn't have to fit nice and neatly in a preexisting space.

Source: Soto, 2012.

Figure 5.5 Frayer Model With Target Phrase: Garden Layout

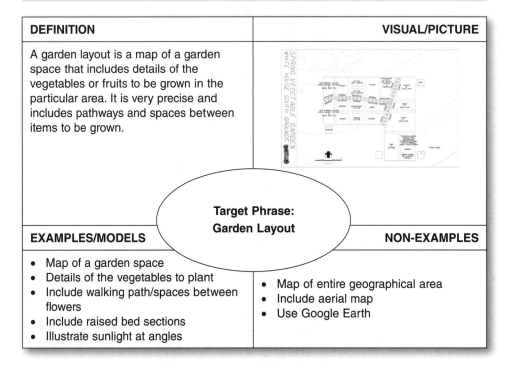

DEFINITION	VISUAL/PICTURE
A garden layout is a map of a garden space that includes details of the vegetables or fruits to be grown in the particular area. It is very precise and includes pathways and spaces between items to be grown.	

Target Phrase: Garden Layout

EXAMPLES/MODELS	NON-EXAMPLES
• Map of a garden space • Details of the vegetables to plant • Include walking path/spaces between flowers • Include raised bed sections • Illustrate sunlight at angles	• Map of entire geographical area • Include aerial map • Use Google Earth

Figure 5.6 Think-Pair-Share Organizer 2: Garden Unit

Question (Open-ended)	What I Think (Speaking)	What My Partner Thought (Listening)	What We Thought (Consensus)
After reviewing the White House garden layout, what kind of layout do you visualize for our school garden?	I think that we need to go measure the space for our garden, and determine the amount of sunlight that the garden receives.	I agree with you, and I wonder how and when we can test the soil health.	We both seem to be interested in the science part of the garden. We can't wait to start measuring sunlight and space.

same website listed under the heading "Eat Healthy" that is titled *MyPlate* and represents the new Food Pyramid. Initially, most students give personal reasons for wanting to grow certain vegetables, so it is up to the teacher to make certain that they are also making healthy and balanced choices for vegetable selections for the school garden. This process allows students to further see the linkage between what they are growing and what they are eating every day. Additionally, this requires students to make evidence-based decisions about their food growing and consuming, instead of merely based on personal preferences. For example, when students read the *Let's Move!* School Garden Checklist, they realize that they must take into consideration soil health (note that this is one of the Frayer model unit words), as well as size, shape, and climate for their garden selections. Furthermore, as students review the *MyPlate* and *MyFood-a-pedia* sources, they begin to see the connections between what they grow and how to maintain a healthy diet, where fruits and vegetables comprise half of their plates. MyFood-a-pedia is a mobile tool (app) to provide consumers quick access to nutrition information (United States Department of Agriculture [USDA], 2010). Figure 5.7 depicts a possible student conversation after studying this extensive research.

Extending Writing With Think-Pair-Share

Notice that in order to build background knowledge around garden content, the Think-Pair-Share graphic organizer was used three times. Students can then use the conversations and notes that they took on this organizer to write their informational essay about the benefits and elements of developing a school garden. In this way, the graphic organizer becomes an outline for their writing so that the conversations are leveraged into extended writing selections. In essence, each question that was considered during the Think-Pair-Share exchange can be extended and turned into a paragraph. All three questions eventually become the informational essay about developing a school garden. See below how the first Think-Pair-Share exchange can become the introductory paragraph to an informational essay.

Figure 5.7 Think-Pair-Share Organizer 3: Garden Unit

Question (Open-ended)	What I Think (Speaking)	What My Partner Thought (Listening)	What We Thought (Consensus)
What kinds of fruits and/or vegetables do you want to plant? Do they connect to the MyPlate Food Pyramid and how?	I believe that we should grow onions and red and green peppers because this is what my mom uses in the kitchen.	I agree with you, Juan, but my mom also uses chayote and potatoes, so I want to make sure that we also include those vegetables.	It seems like both of us want vegetables that our moms use. How about if we branch out with some of the vegetables that were in the White House garden?

Sample Introductory Paragraph

Garden spaces can be developed in unlikely places. For example, the High Line in Manhattan, New York, is an abandoned railway that was repurposed into an urban garden space. At my school site, my class along with the Master Gardener will look for the best space on campus for a garden to be built and develop a garden layout for that space. In order to do this, my class will take into account some scientific concepts, including the amount of sunlight and the soil health. In the paragraphs that follow, I will describe each of these steps in depth using supporting materials that I have read.

Notice how the student leveraged the language and content that was previously introduced in order to fully develop an introductory paragraph for the informational essay on school gardens. Also observe how the student integrated one of the Frayer model target phrases for this unit, *garden layout,* because the words were contextualized and defined for the ELL. Using the Think-Pair-Share exchanges labeled #2, #3, and #4, the student can then follow this introduction with paragraphs that further expand on the topic subject.

Conclusion

The heart of this book is to make the rigorous expectations of the CCSS reasonable and accessible to teachers in the field. It is important to note that some of the same strategies that teachers are already using, especially strategies for Academic Language Development (ALD), can be leveraged into writing scaffolds with ELLs and all other students with access to the CCSS. All of the strategies suggested in this book are included in the Appendices that follow. I encourage teachers to begin developing their own lessons using the Curriculum Cycle lesson plan organizer, as well as incorporating the ALD strategies into their teaching. The lessons included in this book are intended to be sample lessons that can be modified for different grade levels, and serve as examples of what can be done using both the lesson plan organizer and ALD strategies in combination.

The CCSS Standards provide an important opportunity for educators to once again be creative in their curricular designs. Gone are the days of lockstep and formulaic teaching. With this progress comes the responsibility to design experiences for ELLs, as well as all students, to truly understand content and language in an in-depth way. Our ELLs should be doing the heavy lifting and thinking within the CCSS; they should be tired when they leave our classrooms. We have been doing the thinking for them for much too long, and now is the time to release the cognitive work to the ELLs so that they have a fighting chance to succeed in school and beyond. As teachers, we can do the heavy lifting in the design of our curriculum, and in ensuring that it comes to fruition when in the classroom. We must be comfortable with leading from behind, appropriately scaffolding the rigors of the CCSS, and watching our ELLs blossom in the classroom setting. I truly believe that the CCSS, when implemented in conjunction with sound professional development, can provide the access to college and career expectations that so many of our ELLs desperately need to be successful in school, higher education, and beyond.

Appendices

THINK-PAIR-SHARE ORGANIZER WITH ACADEMIC LANGUAGE STEMS

Open-ended Question or Prompt	What I Thought (Speaking)	What My Partner Thought (Listening)	What We Will Share (Consensus)

Source: Soto-Hinman & Hetzel, 2009.

Academic Language Stems

Academic language stems for speaking: "*What I thought was . . . because . . .*"
Academic language stem for listening: "*What my partner thought was . . . because . . .*"
Academic language stem for consensus: "*What we thought was . . . because . . .*"

LANGUAGE STRATEGIES FOR ACTIVE CLASSROOM PARTICIPATION

Expressing an Opinion	Predicting
I think/believe that . . .	I guess/predict/imagine that . . .
It seems to me that . . .	Based on . . . , I infer that . . .
In my opinion . . .	I hypothesize that . . .
Asking for Clarification	**Paraphrasing**
What do you mean?	So you are saying that . . .
Will you explain that again?	In other words, you think . . .
I have a question about that.	What I hear you saying is . . .
Soliciting a Response	**Acknowledging Ideas**
What do you think?	My idea is similar to/related to _____'s idea.
We haven't heard from you yet.	
Do you agree?	I agree with (a person) that . . .
What answer did you get?	My idea builds on _____'s idea.
Reporting a Partner's Idea	**Reporting a Group's Idea**
_____ indicated that . . .	We decided/agreed that . . .
_____ pointed out to me that . . .	We concluded that . . .
_____ emphasized that . . .	Our group sees it differently.
_____ concluded that . . .	We had a different approach.
Disagreeing	**Offering a Suggestion**
I don't agree with you because . . .	Maybe we could . . .
I got a different answer than you.	What if we . . .
I see it another way.	Here's something we might try.
Affirming	**Holding the Floor**
That's an interesting idea.	As I was saying, . . .
I hadn't thought of that.	If I could finish my thought . . .
I see what you mean.	What I was trying to say was . . .

Source: Adapted from Feldman & Kinsella, 2006.

PARTNER CHANT: THINK-PAIR-SHARE

Eye to eye

Knee to knee

Sit right here and learn from me

We'll speak with voices polite indeed

To share our thinking

About books we read

Our partner's thoughts can help us learn

The signal will tell us

It's time to turn

Source: Mesa, 2011.

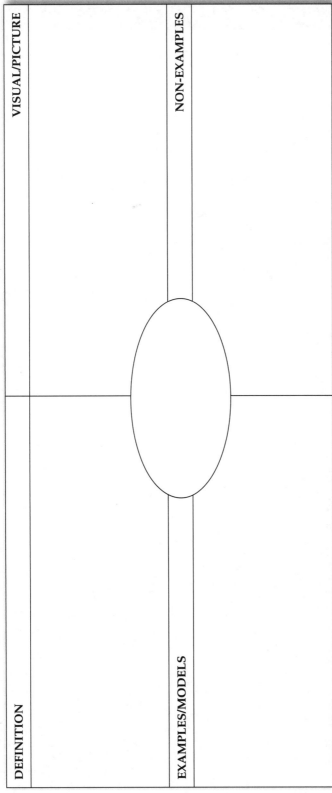

FRAYER MODEL

DEFINITION	VISUAL/PICTURE
EXAMPLES/MODELS	NON-EXAMPLES

Directions: You assume responsibility for helping your group use one of four reading strategies to discuss the assigned reading lesson: summarizing, questioning, predicting, and connecting. As you read, take notes based on your assigned strategy and be prepared to lead a discussion for your role in your group.

Source: Frayer, 1969.

Name: _____   Period: _____

Directions: You will assume the responsibility for helping your group to use one of four reading strategies to discuss the assigned reading: summarizing, questioning, predicting, and connecting. As you read, take notes based on your assigned strategy and be prepared to lead a discussion for your role in your group.

Summarizing	Questioning	Predicting	Connecting
Beyond retelling what happens in the reading, identify what you think are the three most important events/details from the reading and explain why they are important and how they are connected.	Pose at least three questions about the reading; these could include questions that address confusing parts of the reading, or thought questions that the reading makes you wonder about.	Identify at least three text-related predictions; these predictions should be based on new developments in the reading and your predictions should help the group to anticipate what happens next.	Make at least three connections between ideas or events in the reading to your own experience, the world around you, or other texts. Be prepared to explain these connections to your group.

CURRICULUM CYCLE LESSON PLAN ORGANIZER

Common Core State Standard	
Writing Objective	
Building Background Knowledge for Content of Writing	
Specialized Vocabulary Needed (Frayer model)	
Academic Oral Language Development (Think-Pair-Share With Open-ended Questions)	
Purpose	
Organization	
Connectives	
Other Linguistic Features	

Source: Soto, 2012.

EIGHT CHARACTERISTICS OF PRODUCTIVE/EFFECTIVE GROUP WORK CHECKLIST

☐ Clear and explicit instructions are provided.

_____

_____

☐ Talk is necessary for the task.

_____

_____

☐ There is a clear outcome.

_____

_____

☐ The task is cognitively appropriate.

_____

_____

☐ The task is integrated with the broader topic.

_____

_____

☐ All children are involved.

_____

_____

☐ Students have enough time.

_____

_____

☐ Students know how to work in groups.

_____

_____

_____

Source: Adapted from Carstens (in Gibbons, 2002).

References

Achieve. (2013). *Next generation science standards*. Washington, DC: Author.

August, D., & Shanahan, T. (2006). *Developing literacy in second-language learners: Report of the national literacy panel on language minority children and youth.* Mahwah, NJ: Erlbaum.

Ballantyne, K. G., Sanderman, A. R., Levy, J. (2008). *Educating English language learners: Building teacher capacity*. Washington, DC: National Clearinghouse for English Language Acquisition. Available at http://www.ncela.gwu.edu/practice/mainstream_teachers.htm

Beck, I. L., McKeown, M. G., & Kucan, L. (2002). *Bringing words to life: Robust vocabulary instruction*. New York, NY: Guilford Press.

Bloom, B. S., Engelhart, M. D., Furst, E. J., Hill, W. H., & Krathwohl, D. R. (1956). *Taxonomy of educational objectives: The classification of educational goals. Handbook I: Cognitive domain*. New York, NY: David McKay.

Brown, A., & Palincsar, A. (1985). *Reciprocal teaching of comprehension strategies: A natural history of one program for enhancing learning.* Technical Report No. 334. Urbana: University of Illinois Center for the Study of Reading.

Californians Together. (2012). *Raise your voice on behalf of English learners: The English learners and Common Core advocacy toolkit*. Long Beach, CA: Author.

Cannon, J. (1993). *Stellaluna*. New York, NY: Scholastic Press.

Carstens, L. (2003). *Metacomprehension skills across content areas*. PowerPoint Presentation made to District 6. Huntington Park, CA: Los Angeles Unified School District (LAUSD).

Coleman, D. (2012). *Common Core secondary ELA facilitator's guide*. Delaware, MD: Department of Education.

Common Core State Standards. (2013). Retrieved from http://www.corestandards.org

Council of Chief State School Officers. (2012). *Framework for English language proficiency development standards corresponding to the Common Core state standards and the next generation science standards*. Washington, DC: Author.

Education Oasis. (2006). Think-Pair-Share. Hendersonville, North Carolina: Author.

English Online. (2013). *Narrative checklist*. Retrieved from http://www.englishonline.net/

Feldman, K., & Kinsella, K. (2006). *Narrowing the language gap: The case for explicit vocabulary instruction*. New York, NY: Scholastic Press.

Frayer, D. (1969). *Frayer model graphic organizer*. Madison, WI: University of Wisconsin.

Gibbons, P. (2002). *Scaffolding language, scaffolding learning.* Portsmouth, NH: Heinemann.

Goldberger, P. (2011). *Miracle above Manhattan.* Retrieved from http://ngm.nation algeographic.com/2011/04/ny-high-line/goldberger-text

Hakim, J. (2003). A boy with something on his mind. In *A history of US: Finding the stories in science and history.* Oxford, England: Oxford University Press.

Hess, K., Jones, B. S., Carlock, D., & Walkup, J. R. (2009). *Cognitive rigor: Blending the strengths of Bloom's Taxonomy and Webb's Depth-of-Knowledge to enhance classroom-level processes.* [Technical Report ED517804]. Retrieved from ERIC database. Retrieved from http://www.eric.ed.gov/PDFS/ED517804.pdf

High Line in Manhattan. (2011). Elevated park in NYC. Video. *National Geographic Magazine.* Retrieved from http://ngm.nationalgeographic.com/video/player#/?titleID=ny-high-line&catID=1

Israel, E. (2002). Examining multiple perspectives in literature. In J. Holden & J. S. Schmit (Eds.), *Inquiry and the literary text: Constructing discussions in the English classroom.* Urbana, IL: National Council of Teachers of English (NCTE).

Kinsella, K., & Feldman, K. (2005). *Language strategies for active participation and learning.* New York, NY: Scholastic Red. (Presentation made to Mountain View School District, August 2008, Mountain View, CA).

Lee, J. (2009). *Spring gardening.* (White House blog post #9). Retrieved from http://www.whitehouse.gov/blog/09/03/20/Spring-Gardening/ and http://www.gardenorganic.org.uk/growyourown/schools_leaflets.php

Let's Move! (2013). *Eat healthy: MyPlate.* Retrieved from http://www.letsmove.gov/gardening-guide

Let's Move! (2013). *Garden checklist.* Retrieved from http://www.letsmove.gov/gardening-guide

Library of Congress. (2013). *Analyzing primary source documents.* Washington, DC: Author. Retrieved from http://www.loc.gov/teachers/usingprima rysources/

Line, S. (2002). *Persuasive model letter for District 6 secondary unit of study.* Huntington Park, CA: Los Angeles Unified School District (LAUSD).

Linquanti, R., & Hakuta, K. (2012). *How next-generation science standards and assessment can foster success for California's English learners.* Stanford, CA: Policy Analysis for California Education (PACE).

Marzano, R. (2004). *Building background knowledge for academic achievement.* Alexandria, VA: Association for Supervision and Curriculum Development (ASCD).

Mesa, I. (2011). *Partner chant for Think-Pair-Share.* Morrison Elementary School. Retrieved from http://memegenerator.net/

National Governors Association (NGA) Center for Best Practices, & the Council of Chief State School Officers (CCSSO). (2010b). *Common core state standards for English language arts & literacy in history/social studies, science, and technical subjects.* Washington, DC: Author. Retrieved from http://www.corestandards.org/assets/CCSSI_ELA%20Standards.pdf

National Governors Association (NGA) Center for Best Practices, & the Council of Chief State School Officers (CCSSO). (2010c). *common core state standards for math.* Washington, DC: Author. Retrieved from http://www.corestandards.org/assets/CCSSI_ELA%20Standards.pdf

National Governors Association (NGA) Center for Best Practices, & the Council of Chief State School Officers (CCSSO). (2010a). *Common core state standards initiative*. Washington, DC: Author. Retrieved from http://www.corestan dards.org/assets/CCSSI_ELA%20Standards.pdf

(NCLB) No Child Left Behind Act of 2001, Pub Law No. 107–110, § 115 Stat. 1425 (2002, Jan. 8). *The Elementary and Secondary Education Act.* Washington, DC: Government Printing Office.

Public Broadcasting Services. (1997). *Einstein revealed.* Retrieved from http:// www.pbs.org/wgbh/nova/physics/einstein-revealed.html

Rylant, C. (1982). *When I was young in the mountains.* New York, NY: Dutton Children's Books.

Smarter Balanced Assessment Consortium. (2013). Retrieved from http://www .smarterbalanced.org/smarter-balanced-assessments/

Soto, I. (2012). *ELL shadowing as a catalyst for change.* Thousand Oaks, CA: Corwin.

Soto-Hinman, I., & Hetzel, J. (2009). *The literacy gaps: Building bridges for ELLs and SELs.* Thousand Oaks, CA: Corwin.

Understanding Language Initiative. (2012). *Language, literacy, and learning in the content areas.* Stanford, CA: Stanford University. Retrieved from http://ell .stanford.edu/

United States Department of Agriculture. (2010). *Myfood-a-pedia.* Washington, DC: Government Printing Office.

United States Holocaust Memorial Museum. (1995). *Propaganda and primary source documents.* Washington, DC: Author. Retrieved from http://www.ushmm .org/propaganda/

Webb, N. L. (2002). *Depth-of-Knowledge for four content areas.* Retrieved from http://schools.nyc.gov/NR/rdonlyres/2711181C-2108–40C4-A7F8– 76F243C9B910/0/DOKFourContentAreas.pdf

Index

CORWIN
A SAGE Company

The Corwin logo—a raven striding across an open book—represents the union of courage and learning. Corwin is committed to improving education for all learners by publishing books and other professional development resources for those serving the field of PreK–12 education. By providing practical, hands-on materials, Corwin continues to carry out the promise of its motto: **"Helping Educators Do Their Work Better."**